# MEDITATIONS
# ON THE MASS

# MEDITATIONS
## ON THE
# MASS

*by* Bernard C. Mischke, o. s. c.

SHEED AND WARD – NEW YORK

To my father and my mother
Joseph and Margaret Mischke
who first taught me
to love the Mass

# ACKNOWLEDGMENTS

Grateful acknowledgment is made to the following for the use of quoted material:

The Confraternity of Christian Doctrine, for quotations from the Confraternity translation of the Bible.

The *Canadian Messenger* and *The Messenger of the Sacred Heart,* in whose pages many of these meditations have previously appeared.

# PREFACE

The purpose of this little book is to help Christians understand and appreciate more and more the great mystery of the Mass. For if we come to know and love the Mass even to a fraction of what it deserves, we will begin to live the Mass all day long.

This is no great work of scholarship; it is in no sense an adequate treatment of the theological or historical or liturgical aspects of the Mass. It is a collection of thoughts that any Christian trying to take his part in the Mass could work over in his mind and write down on paper.

The form of these meditations is simple. The parts of the Roman Mass are treated in order, prayer by prayer. Each meditation begins with the text of the Mass on which we are meditating; then a text or two from Holy Scripture is given for reflection; some development of a thought on the two texts follows; each of the meditations concludes with another prayer, usually taken from one of the Eucharistic liturgies of the Eastern Church. It is my hope that this method will unfold the beauties and treasures of the texts of the Mass. I believe the background of Holy Scripture and the beautiful prayers of the Eastern Rites will serve well to deepen our appreciation and love of the Holy Sacrifice.

—BCM

# CONTENTS

# THOUGHTS BEFORE MASS

What we do at Mass is the most important work of today or any day. It has a most significant purpose and demands our fullest attention. I say *we*, not *I*. I am not acting alone, but with my parish and my community, for this is our public sacrifice, our united worship and love and prayer.

What I do at Mass now is far more vital than what clever business deal I may make as a breadwinner, or how many good meals I make as a housewife, or how many high marks I get as a student, or how many games I win as an athlete. These things are important only as they reflect what I do at Mass.

Make no mistake: what I do with my talents, what excellence I attain by hard work, what intellectual and spiritual service I am to my neighbor—these are vitally important things! But in true Christian life they must derive their vitality from my actions at the Mass, and conversely, my actions at the Mass derive their vitality from these other duties, from what I am doing for the spread of Christ's kingdom on earth. That is why it is so necessary that I understand the Mass well; it must become fully relevant to my daily life.

At Mass I am not alone; here I am not hiding myself from the world to plunge into a bath of private devotions and personal religious feelings. Love and devotion I may experience, but these will flow from the active part I take with my parish and my whole community in performing this perfect act of praise and thanksgiving and sacrifice. I am one here with the Communion of Saints—the Church in this world and in the next—united in the perfect bond of love, the bond of Jesus Christ.

So here at Mass I am *we,* I am one with Christ and the members of his Mystical Body. We are here to do what is most necessary for ourselves and the whole world around us—we are here to bind ourselves to God.

We all seek "progress." To have real progress we must have pervading peace, justice, and charity. We shall not have these blessings in our homes or communities, or states or nations, unless the service of God is given utmost importance in our private and public life.

Our greatest duty in life is the service of God and neighbor. The service to God is the greater commandment and the duty to neighbor flows out of it. That service is a total dedication, complete commitment, whole-hearted devotion. This we are taught to do in the Mass, where we join with the perfect self-sacrifice of Christ, the primary exemplar of total dedication.

The Mass must reach deeply into our lives if we are to Christianize the world around us. The service of God must be far and away the greatest living force in our daily actions. God himself in the Old Testament condemned the formalistic lip service of his people, who made their sacrifices mere words and ritual with no real meaning. "These people honor me with their lips, but their hearts are far from me," God warned through Isaias. Jesus himself repeated the warning, and strongly attacked the hypocrisy of those who washed the outside of the cup and dish, but inwardly remained dead and rotten.

The Mass is the action of religious men, "God's holy people," uniting themselves with the holiest of the holy, the Son of God made man, Jesus Christ, in whose person the divine and human natures are joined. If we are to be real partakers, then, if we are not to abuse or insult the Holy Sacrifice, we must see to it that we are truly "holy people" and that we are truly "God's people." Blind, weak, twisted sinners that we are, we recognize our frightful un-worthiness. But this can never discourage us from the constant effort to be more worthy of Christ, to be all day long in a true sense the people of God, preparing to offer each day's Mass with greater holiness and love. This is no easy assignment, but the most necessary one of all.

# MEDITATIONS
# ON THE MASS

# I.

## IN HIS NAME

IN THE NAME OF THE FATHER, AND OF THE SON, AND OF THE HOLY SPIRIT. AMEN.

*Go and make disciples of all nations, baptizing them in the name of the Father, and of the Son, and of the Holy Spirit, teaching them to observe all that I have commanded you; and behold, I am with you all days, even unto the consummation of the world.* (Matt. 28:19)

*When the Advocate has come, whom I will send you from the Father, the Spirit of truth who proceeds from the Father, he will bear witness concerning me.* (John 15:26)

*The Holy Spirit, whom the Father will send in my name, will teach you all things, and bring to your mind whatever I have said to you.* (John 14:26)

We begin the great mystery of the Mass by reference to the mystery upon which it is ultimately based. We are reminded immediately that "God so loved the world that he gave his only-begotten Son, that those who believe in him may not perish, but may have life everlasting" (John 3:16). These are the words of Jesus himself.

We begin the Mass with the Sign of the Cross, because it recalls the two most important truths of our faith: the Holy Trinity, and

our redemption in the Cross. We say the names of the persons of
the Divine Trinity, and we trace over ourselves the image of the
Cross. Both mysteries are mysteries of perfect love.

The Holy Trinity is infinitely above our understanding; God
himself is essentially and eternally a mystery beyond our comprehen-
sion. He is not limited by time or space or weakness as we are. His
days of life are not numbered as ours; his power or his love are in
no sense restricted. When we think of God, when we try to see
with our small minds just what he is, we seem constantly to resort
to negatives: he is without evil; no selfishness, no vices of any kind,
no limitations or inadequacies can be found in him. He is all
goodness and all perfection and all existence in himself. If anything
in life is unreal, it is we, not he.

Yet, if we should speak in a very human way of God, we should
say that from nature alone our knowledge of God is somehow im-
personal, cold, and distant. Not that we should fail to discover
personality in God; after all, we know that intellect and will and
the functions of mind make personality in our human life. Is not
God, the supreme mind, all the more personal? But of his inner,
intimate life, we should yet have many unanswered questions. He
would seem (to us) to dwell distant and alone, in awesome silence.

What a glorious revelation, then, when God sends his Son to
live among us, and we find that far from being set apart in loneli-
ness, the eternal Lord of the universe is a family, living together in
the deepest bond of love. What a beautiful and ever widening
mystery is the Holy Trinity! Son proceeding from the Father,
divine and glorious expression of the Father's mind; Holy Spirit
proceeding from the love of Father and Son. Divine model for all
love and friendship and unity and cooperation on earth.

And for us, what a glorious revelation when the Son becomes a
member of our human family, thus joining us mysteriously to the
divine family! The Cross is the great bridge from earth to heaven,
bringing men from all parts of the earth, and raising them heavenward, as Christ Jesus was raised on the Cross. "If I be lifted up, I
will draw all things to myself." As all things were drawn up to

God on the Cross, so now are all things drawn up to him in the Mass, the renewal of the Cross.

It is altogether fitting and beautiful that we begin the Mass with the names of the Holy Trinity, the divine family in which we have received an adopted membership, and with the Sign of the Cross, which has drawn us up to the heavenly family.

*Prayer: We worship you, Christ, with your excellent Father and the Holy Spirit, as we say, you have come to us; you have redeemed us. Have mercy on us. Almighty God, all-holy Trinity, Lord God of armies, stay with us. Truly, in our sorrows and trials, we have no other hope but you....*

*In the name of the Father and of the Son and of the Holy Spirit. Blessed be God, the almighty Father. Amen. Blessed be his only Son, our Lord Jesus Christ. Amen. Blessed be the Holy Spirit, our Comforter. Amen. Glory and honor be to the most holy Trinity, Father, Son, and Holy Spirit....*

*One holy Father, one holy Son, one Holy Spirit. Amen. Blessed be the Lord God for all ages. Amen.*

(*Opening Prayers of the Coptic Liturgy*)

## 2.

## JUDGE ME

Judge me, O God, and defend my cause against a faithless people; from the deceitful and impious man, rescue me. For you, my God, are my strength; why do you keep me so far away? Why must I go about in mourning, with the enemy oppressing me? Send forth your light and your fidelity; they shall lead me on and bring me to your holy mountain, to your dwelling-place. Then will I go in to the altar of God, the God of my gladness and joy; then will I give you thanks on the harp, O God, my God! Why are you so downcast, my soul? Why do you sigh within me? Hope in God! For I shall again be thanking him in the presence of my savior and my God. (Psalm 42)

*They who shall choose the things that please me, and shall hold fast my covenant, I will give them a place in my house, and a name better than sons and daughters. I will give them an everlasting name which shall never perish. . . . I will bring them into my holy mount, and will make them joyful in my house of prayer. Their holocausts and their offerings shall please me upon my altar, for my house shall be called the house of prayer, for all nations. (Isaias 56:4, 7)*

It is likely enough that the Church has kept Psalm 42 as the introductory prayer of the Mass because of its verse, "I will go up

to the altar of God, the God of my joy and gladness." The Mass
is a joyous festival, though it commemorates and re-enacts a death
and a self-sacrifice which we humans too often consider stark
tragedy, surrounded by forboding gloom. There is an aura of sorrow
around the crucifix, too, when we consider how many souls have
ignored the love that it proved. All the more when we see in every
age—particularly ours—that millions of new crucifixes are raised,
bearing on them the martyred saints. Mankind has not yet learned
its lesson; other Christs are persecuted, as he was. Yet the more
powerful effect is that of rejoicing, over the victory of love and
sacrifice.

But there is much more in this first psalm of the Mass (there are
many more selections from that poetic book in the Mass, both in
the Ordinary and the Propers of the Mass) worth notice and meditation. . . .

"Do me justice, O God, and fight my battle against a faithless
people." Here is the very kind of hyperbole that we need at the
beginning of Mass, the kind of ironic note on which we might begin
our worship of God with great profit. We Christians, so often self-
justified, smug and pleased with the few good works we do—"we
are Church-goers and we give to charity"—full of prejudices and
narrowness and often downright hatreds, perhaps firmly anchored
in favorite forms of deceit and malicious practices toward our
neighbor—yes, with great fear and trembling and sad irony, we can
attempt to pray with the saints of God, the martyrs in agony. Who
else can say these words in their fullest meaning but the martyrs?
This is a psalm for the persecuted just man.

Very well, it shall be an excellent way to judge our worthiness,
and thus it shall prepare us for a deep, sincere admission of fault
in the *Confiteor,* the confession we are about to make. It is wise for
the Church first to give us this psalm of justification, as a mirror
in which we may see our true selves, and have true cause to share
deeply in the coming prayers for mercy—the confession, the absolution, and the *Kyrie,* Lord have mercy.

"From the deceitful and impious man rescue me." A three-fold request, when closely examined. We ask, on the surface, to be spared the material losses and sufferings that many suffer at the hands of criminals—often unsuspected thieves or persecutors who are too clever to be caught in their false dealings and slanders. We ask, quite as clearly, to be spared the spiritual harm of bad example. Christ warned us that "because evil would abound, the charity of many would grow cold." From the harm of scandal, the evil of being led into sin by deceitful and impious strategies, we also beg to be rescued. But most of all, we need to be saved from ourselves. From being myself an impious and deceitful man, O Lord, rescue me. For if any evil remains entrenched in my heart as I approach this altar, of what benefit will this holy altar be to me?

> This above all, to thine ownself be true
> And it must follow, as the night the day,
> Thou canst not then be false to any man. (*Hamlet* I, iii)

If only I do not deceive myself, if only I do not become smug in hypocrisy, if only I trust in God rather than in my own desires, I can be led "to your holy mountain."

Deliver me, Lord, from my impieties, that I may "go up to the altar of God," cleansed and repentant, and then you can be the "God who gives me joy and gladness."

*Prayer: I will go up to the altar of God, to God who has brought gladness to my youth. O God, I have entered your house, I have knelt down before your throne: O Heavenly King, forgive me all my offences against you....*

*Lord, you love the sinner who repents; may you accept the fragrant incense offered you by the faithful sons and daughters of the Church through the hands of the priests. . . . O Lord of all holiness, Lord most strong, Lord the immortal One, have mercy on us. . . . May grace and mercy come down upon us, the weak and sinful, now and always and for all time, in this world and in the next.*

*(Opening Prayers from the Maronite Liturgy)*

# 3.

## I CONFESS

I CONFESS TO ALMIGHTY GOD, TO BLESSED MARY EVER VIRGIN, TO
BLESSED MICHAEL THE ARCHANGEL, TO BLESSED JOHN THE BAPTIST, TO
THE HOLY APOSTLES PETER AND PAUL, TO ALL THE SAINTS AND TO YOU,
BROTHERS (AND TO YOU, FATHER) THAT I HAVE SINNED GREATLY IN
THOUGHT, WORD, AND ACTION—THROUGH MY FAULT, THROUGH MY
FAULT, THROUGH MY OWN MOST SERIOUS FAULT. AND SO I BEG BLESSED
MARY EVER VIRGIN, BLESSED MICHAEL THE ARCHANGEL, BLESSED JOHN
THE BAPTIST, THE HOLY APOSTLES PETER AND PAUL, ALL THE SAINTS AND
YOU, BROTHERS (AND YOU, FATHER) TO PRAY FOR ME TO THE LORD OUR
GOD.

*They will have to confess that they and their fathers were guilty
of having rebelled against me and of having defied me, so that
I, too, had to defy them and bring them into their enemies' land.
Then, when their uncircumcised hearts are humbled and they make
amends for their guilt, I will remember my covenant with Jacob,
my covenant with Isaac, and my covenant with Abraham. . . . Yet
even so, even while they are in their enemies' land, I will not
reject or spurn them, lest, by wiping them out, I make void my
covenant with them; for I, the Lord, am their God. (Leviticus
26:40)*

*Confess your sins to one another, and pray for one another, that
you may be saved. (James 5:16)*

9

This great act of contrition is a preparation for our final judgment. The confession places us before the most august members of the heavenly court—God, the all-powerful, first of all. To him all our actions, all our innermost thoughts and desires, all our most secret self-deceits are seen constantly in brightest day.

We humble ourselves before God, but this is easy enough, in one sense. No sane man considers himself superior to God. Kings who claimed divine rights, emperors and presidents and all the greatest have acknowledged that they must bow down before the Lord of the universe.

The greater humility is in admitting our wretchedness before our fellowmen. Before all the saints of heaven, before Mary and John the Baptist and the great Apostles and all the holy ones, we acknowledge our sinfulness and our consequent unworthiness.

This is not yet enough. We are Christians on earth, here in this community, here with these clear responsibilities toward our brethren who kneel around us, and to all the others who live around us. We owe much to them, but we have failed them. We owe them a confession, too. Therefore we pray "to all the saints and to you, brothers," that we have sinned greatly in our thoughts, in our talk, in our selfish actions.

Our own willful pride, our self-developed corruption, our blindness are the cause of our selfishness. We are in great need of help. We have not succeeded on the strength of our own goodness, and that is not surprising. There is no pattern of godliness or justice or love or peace or holiness outside of God. We have been too convinced of our own excellence, ignoring God, looking for happiness without him, taking credit for every accomplishment as though it were the work of our own power; then as we have failed, we have condemned others in order to spare ourselves.

Now, at the altar of truth, at the sight of Christ's sacrifice for us, for once we intend to be honest. Honesty with God is the foundation of all true reform. We are at fault, Lord, grievously at fault. We are sinful members of a sinful race. Nevertheless, we cannot be so slothful as to accept that shocking confession as a matter of course. It will not do to sink back into the unprofitable sleep out of which we have here and now by your grace emerged. We must make concrete reparation, we must cleanse ourselves "from dead works," and become alive to God. For this task we are in need of much help—God's grace, most of all, and the prayerful support of our fellow-Christians. "Therefore we beg blessed Mary . . . and all the saints . . . and you, brothers (and you, Father) to pray to the Lord our God for us."

*Prayer: Lord, accept our prayers through the mediation of the holy mother of God, spotless mother of your only Son, and through the mediation of all the saints. Listen kindly to us and have pity on us, Lord; pardon us; show your generous mercy to us, wipe out our sins, and make us worthy to give glory to you in union with your Son and the Holy Spirit, now and for all ages. I confess to God, in the presence of his holy mother, in the presence of all the saints and of you, fathers and brethren; I confess all the sins I have committed. For I have been a sinner in thought, word, and action, in whatever ways men are prone to sin. I have sinned, I have indeed sinned, and I beseech you to ask forgiveness of God for me.*

*(Opening Prayer, Armenian Liturgy)*

# 4.

## LORD, HAVE MERCY

MAY GOD, THE ALL-POWERFUL AND ALL-MERCIFUL, GRANT US PARDON, ABSOLUTION, AND FORGIVENESS OF OUR SINS. AMEN.

O GOD, YOU WILL TURN TO US AND GIVE US LIFE: AND YOUR PEOPLE WILL FIND JOY IN YOU.

SHOW US, LORD, YOUR GRACIOUS MERCY: AND SEND US YOUR SALVATION.

LORD, LISTEN TO MY PRAYER: AND LET MY PLEADING REACH YOUR EARS.

THE LORD IS WITH YOU: AND WITH YOUR SPIRIT.

*Let the wicked forsake his way, and the unjust man his thoughts, and let him return to the Lord, and he will have mercy on him; let him return to our God, for he is bountiful to forgive. (Isaias 55:7)*

*Let all bitterness and wrath, and indignation, and clamor, and reviling be removed from you, along with all malice. On the contrary, be kind to one another and merciful, generously forgiving one another, as also God in Christ has generously forgiven you. (Ephesians 4:32)*

Our sin is recognized, our fault is admitted, our guilt is confessed. We know that we "have sinned exceedingly in thought, word, and deed." We are unworthy to rise and go up to the altar of God. We ought not to stay here; our sins have made us unfit to offer this sublime gift. We must agree with Shakespeare "that in the course

*12*

of justice, none of us should see salvation," but we also agree with him further that "we do pray for mercy; and that same prayer doth teach us all to render the deeds of mercy."

At the beginning of the Mass we must remember that God's dealings with his people are an endless series of mercies. It is important for us to know it; it is important for us to pray for those mercies. We understand well that we have no reason to come before God boasting or demanding rewards. We have been more than rewarded; we are the most fortunate of beggars; we are in no way worthy of the gifts he continues to surround us with:

May the almighty and merciful Lord grant us pardon. . . .
Show us your mercy, Lord, and grant us your salvation. . . .
Lord have mercy on us. . . . Christ have mercy. . . . Lord have mercy. . . .

His mercy, the psalmist assures us, "is high as heaven," though ours is small and corrupt. His mercy is selfless and generous; ours is proud and political. His mercy had nothing to expect from us, for his mercy created us, raised us up when we had fallen hopelessly, spared us from the punishments we deserved.

These opening prayers for mercy ought to remind us how God has dealt with us, and how he asks us to deal with our neighbor in turn. "If you forgive others, your heavenly Father will forgive you, but if you do not forgive men, neither will your Father forgive you your offenses." So in begging for your mercy, Lord, we also pray for the wisdom to exercise mercy where we ought.

What warped, twisted, irrational prayer would these pleas for mercy be, if we did not sincerely intend to practice the mercy for which we asked you. We hope to share God's heaven, we desire his happiness, we want his blessing and approval, we pray that his justice be done, but we will have so little of his mercy. The slightest offense forgiven seems to us a magnificent outburst of mercy. Revenge, we think, is necessary to maintain our superior position. We think of mercy as a weakness, as the inability to "stand up for one's rights." And because we have so little understanding of this great virtue, and so little respect for it, we abuse the mercy that others show to us. We imagine that we have "gotten away with" our injustices and offenses. We give no credit to the patience and forgiveness of those we imagine to have "defeated."

Such is the sorry state of our mercy, Lord, and of our respect for mercy. Yet if we know you at all, should we not expect that when we fail to imitate your mercy, when we take advantage of those who exercise mercy on us, we may hear you speak to us one day, "I am Jesus, whom you persecute. . . . What you have done to the least of these, My brethren, you have done to Me"?

*Prayer: May the all-powerful God grant you mercy and pardon all your sins, past and present, and keep you far from them in the days to come; may he give you strength in all good works and bring you to eternal peace after this life. Amen.*

*May the Lord God, lover of all men, set you free from all your sins and grant you forgiveness; may he bless you with time to do penance and every good work. May the almighty and ever-merciful God guide you throughout your life by the loving grace of his Holy Spirit. To him be praise through everlasting time. Amen.*

*(**Preparation Prayers, Armenian Liturgy**)*

# 5.

## WITH SOULS MADE CLEAN

REMOVE OUR SINS FROM US, LORD, WE BEG YOU, SO THAT WITH SOULS
MADE CLEAN, WE MAY BE FOUND WORTHY TO PASS INTO THE HOLY OF
HOLIES: THROUGH CHRIST OUR LORD. AMEN.

WE ASK YOU, LORD, THROUGH THE GOOD WORKS OF YOUR SAINTS,
WHOSE RELICS ARE HERE BEFORE US, THAT BECAUSE OF YOUR GOODNESS
YOU WILL PARDON ALL MY SINS. AMEN.

*Have mercy on me, O God, in your goodness; in the greatness
of your compassion wipe out my offense. Thoroughly wash me from
my guilt and of my sin cleanse me.* (Psalm 50:3–4)

*The souls of the just are in the hands of God. . . . For if before
men, indeed, they be punished, yet is their hope full of immortality;
chastised a little, they shall be greatly blessed, because God tried
them and found them worthy of himself. As gold in the furnace, he
proved them, and as sacrificial offerings he took them to himself. . . .
They shall judge nations and rule over peoples, and the Lord shall be
their King forever.* (Wisdom 3:1, 4–8)

At the foot of the altar, we have confessed our unworthiness to
offer so great a gift as the Mass. We have been reminded of God's
infinite mercy—infinite, and thus able to cover all our need of mercy.
We have sinned; we have marred and effaced the image of God

in us, if indeed we have not destroyed it time and again by mortal sin, an open rebellion.

In the Sacrament of Penance, God has forgiven us. Even so, we are crippled by sin, we are left in a kind of ruin; sin has devoured us like a cancer; we are weak and a relapse will be all too easy. That is why we pray, "Remove our sins from us, Lord, we beg . . . that we may be found worthy to pass into the holy of holies." We say it with the priest, as we ascend the altar with him.

Why the repeated reference to our sins and unworthiness? Because we want to take a *real* part in the Mass. We do not look upon the Mass as some artificial drama, during which for the time being we can forget our true position before God. We do not consider the Mass as some kind of blanket with which our spiritual decay can be temporarily covered. We cannot conquer evil by hiding it; closing our eyes to wickedness only gives it a better chance to grow.

And so throughout the Mass we ask God to cleanse us of evil, to take away our sins, to deliver us from them—not to ignore them or to minimize them. We wish to be a real part of the Holy Sacrifice, and to be so, we must share the innocence of Christ, our Sacrifice.

We know in coming to the Mass that here is Calvary's redemption renewed. We know, too, that Jesus did not undergo the torments of the Cross for some small, artificial cause, nor does he renew that sacrifice on the altar as mere religious drama.

If we are participants in the Mass, it is not in the sense that Christ covers us with his holiness as a white sheet might cover a corpse from view. Rather, he offers himself to cure us of our corruption, to be our medicine, to reach into us down to the marrow of our bones, to cut out and take out our sins, to take all sinful desires and weaknesses out of our hearts, and to replace them with spiritual health. We accept no ideal less than this.

The Mass is our Sacrament of Strength. It is real, it truly unites us to Christ. We not only receive Christ bodily at the Communion;

we put on the mind of Christ throughout the Mass. This is the fact
on which the opening prayers of the Mass insist.

*Prayer: Holy God, you live among the saints, you are praised by
the Seraphim and glorified by the Cherubim in the thrice-holy
hymn, you are worshipped by all the powers of heaven; you
brought all creation out of emptiness into being and fashioned man
according to your own image and likeness and adorned him with
all the beauties of your grace. You give wisdom and understanding
to whoever asks for them; you do not turn your back on the sinner,
but you offer him repentance to save him. You have allowed us
feeble and unworthy servants to stand now before the majesty of
your sacred altar and offer you fitting adoration and honor.*

*O Lord, accept even from the lips of sinners such as we, the
thrice-holy song of praise, and mercifully bend down to us. Forgive us every sin and fault, whether committed out of willfulness
or weakness. Purify our souls and bodies, and strengthen us to serve
you as we ought, all the days that we may live. We ask this through
the prayers of the holy Mother of God and of all the Saints who have
served you most faithfully through the ages of time.*

*(Prayer of the Little Entrance, Byzantine Liturgy)*

# 6.

## ENTRANCE SONG

(A PSALM OR TEXT THAT VARIES WITH THE FEAST OR THE SEASON.)

*Sing joyfully to the Lord. . . .Come before him with joyful song. Know that the Lord is God; he made us, his we are; his people, the flock he tends. Enter his gates with thanksgiving, his courts with praise; give thanks to him; bless his name, for he is good: the Lord, whose kindness endures forever, and his faithfulness, to all generations. (Psalm 99)*

*Those times I recall now that I pour out my soul within me, when I went with the throng and led them in procession to the house of God, amid loud cries of joy and thanksgiving, with the multitude keeping festival. (Psalm 41:5)*

In a full-fledged celebration of the Holy Sacrifice, a sung Mass, the song of entrance really begins the Mass. It presumes a solemn procession to the altar, during which the "introit" is a song that sets the mood of the festive occasion—for the Mass is a feast. (We have placed the entrance song here because of the place it occupies in printed missals.)

For great feasts, the tone of the entrance hymn is unequivocally joyous and victorious. Such, for example, are the Resurrection of Christ: "I have arisen and I am still with you, alleluia!" Pentecost, the Coming of the Holy Spirit: "The Spirit of the Lord has filled the whole earth, alleluia!" Christmas Day: "A Child is born to us

and a Son is given us!" The Feast of All Saints: "Let us all rejoice
in the Lord, keeping holiday to honor all the saints."

Often the mood of the entry is mysteriously paradoxical in ac-
cordance with the meaning of the feast itself, such as the commemoration of the martyrdom of a saint. It is a strange and inexpressibly
beautiful blend of sadness and joy, sorrow at the unjust persecution
of the saint, and joy at the couragous constancy of the saint. "Let
the groaning of the prisoner ascend before you, Lord; pay back
our neighbors sevenfold into their hearts; revenge the blood of
your saints that has been shed." In the light of the joyous tone of
martyrs' Masses, this becomes a song of love and mercy. Because
of the present glory and joy of the martyrs, the mood of vengeance
is one of merciful vegeance, a desire to cleanse and pardon the earth
by this holy blood.

Such, too, is the poignant mood of Holy Thursday, with its
combined depths of sorrow and of joy: "It is for us to glory in the
Cross of our Lord Jesus Christ, for there is our salvation, our life
and resurrection; through Him we have been saved and given
freedom." Or the entrance hymn at the beginning of the penitential
season, Septuagesima Sunday: "The terrors of death surrounded
me, the sorrows of the grave overtook me. In my distress I called
upon the Lord; from his temple he heard my voice. I love you,
O Lord, my strength; O Lord, my rock of refuge, my shield, my
deliverer."

The changing propers—hymns and lessons—of the Mass lend
special fullness and glory to the Holy Sacrifice. They unveil the
Mass's special power to fit every occasion in the lives of Christians.
The Mass is always "the right place for Christians to be," in joy
and sorrow, in victory or defeat, in the happiest occasions of our
earthly life or the most mournful. Always, there is the beauty of
restraint and balance, the understanding and the willing acceptance
of the sons of God.

We are not overwhelmed and crushed by the grief of death in
our midst. We sorrow, but are strong in our faith and confidence;
thus the entrance hymn, "Eternal rest grant them, O Lord, and let
the light eternal shine upon them," is a most touching tribute to

the Church's and the Christian's position between earth and heaven.
"We have here no lasting city," says the introit. "Our goal is the
world to come." What genuine comfort and calm reassurance for
Christians in that entrance hymn of the funeral Mass!

Even the Introit of the year's feast of most explosive triumph
and jubilation is one of calm and serene confidence, restrained and
quiet: "I have arisen and am still with you, alleluia!" It is the
serene voice of the Lord, the voice we can recognize as the apostle
John did on the Sea of Galilee after Christ's Resurrection, the
voice that bids us have no fear, for he is with us at all times, living
forever.

The entrance hymn opens the day's meditation. It is poetic and
thought-provoking, alive with the feeling of the season and the
meaning of specific feast days. It is beautifully reflective of the
meaning of the whole Christian life, as the very life of Christ and
the living calendar of the Church grow towards both death and
resurrection, toward both total self-surrender and total finding of
self, total sacrifice and total reward, complete conformity to the
spirit of Christ Jesus, who assured us of the mysterious paradox
that our faith would be: "He who loses his life for my sake will
secure it forever."

*Prayer: Open to me the gates of justice; I will enter them and
give thanks to the Lord. This gate is the Lord's; the just shall enter
it. I will give thanks to you, for you have answered me and have
been my savior. The stone which the builders rejected has become
the cornerstone. By the Lord has this been done; it is wonderful
in our eyes. This is the day the Lord has made; let us be glad and
rejoice in it. . . .*

*The Lord is God, and he has given us light. Join in procession
with leafy boughs up to the horns of the altar. You are my God and
I give thanks to you; O my God, I extol you. Give thanks to the
Lord, for he is good; for his kindness endures forever.*

*(Psalm 117)*

# 7.

## KYRIE ELEISON

LORD, HAVE MERCY. . . . CHRIST, HAVE MERCY. . . . LORD, HAVE MERCY. . . .

*"O Lord, have pity on me; heal me, though I have sinned against you." (Psalm 40:5)*

*May God have pity on us and bless us; may he let his face shine upon us. (Psalm 66:2)*

*Behold, as the eyes of servants are on the hands of their masters, as the eyes of a maid are on the hands of her mistress, so are our eyes on the Lord, our God, till he have pity on us. Have pity on us, O Lord, have pity on us, for we are more than sated with contempt. (Psalm 122)*

The Mass is not a pious Lethe, a stream of oblivion in which our past or our daily problems or the confusion of the world outside is obliterated for a merciful hour, as though it were a time of religious recreation. Rather, it is the most important work of the day, a total sacrifice in which everything else acquires its real meaning, and to which the world around us must be brought and healed. We have very much to pray for at the Mass, many friends and many enemies to remember, many petitions to present to the throne, for we *belong* to all creation and are responsible for it. It is true that we need a certain and very definite detachment from creation in order to love God rightly, but that detachment frees us from the wrong, abusive, destructive love of created goods. It does not by any means free us from the love of creation; rather, it demands that we love creatures, but love them truly and rightly. Detachment is a correct *ordering* of love; it teaches us to love genuinely; it never cuts us off from love.

That is why the Mass has from its very beginnings included many petitions for the Christian's fellowmen, for the blessings of God to bring forth fruits and crops in abundance, to free man from all kinds of calamities, to change the hearts of persecutors and all evildoers, to guide ecclesiastical and civil rulers toward just government, in a word, to give more and more spiritual strength to weakened mankind.

The Kyrie of the Roman Mass is a remnant of these earlier litanies of petitions. Such requests in litany form are still found in nearly all the Eastern liturgies. A fine example (of the many) of the Church's concern for the world around her when she offered the Holy Sacrifice is found in a fifth century litany of the Western liturgy, a Roman litany ascribed to Pope Gelasius; among its petitions are these:

Lord, have mercy on us and hear us.

For the unblemished Church of the living God, throughout the world in all places, we petition the Lord God, the treasure of all goodness.

Kyrie eleison.

For the holy priests of the all-holy God, those who minister at his holy altar, and all people who are worshippers of the true God, we send up our prayers to our Lord, Christ.

Kyrie eleison.

For those who fulfill their duty of preaching the words of truth, we pray most earnestly to the Word of God in his boundless wisdom.

Kyrie eleison.

For those who keep themselves pure in soul and body for the sake of the kingdom of heaven and spend themselves in spiritual good works, we pray to him who gives spiritual graces.

Kyrie eleison.

For Christian princes and their armies, such as love justice and upright dealings, we pray to God, the all-powerful.

Kyrie eleison.

For mild and health-giving weather, for rain at the right seasons, for gentle, invigorating winds, and for the good ordering of the seasons, we beg the Lawgiver of the universe.

Kyrie eleison.

We beg the omnipotent God to shower his mercy on those who have begun to learn of Christianity and who have begun to desire its heavenly grace.

Kyrie eleison.

We beg the Redeemer of mankind to shower his mercy on all who suffer the weaknesses common to human nature, on those suffering from the wickedness of evil spirits or from errors found in the world.

Kyrie eleison.

We beseech our Lord and Savior to have mercy on all who are forced to live in exile, all who suffer from the unjust persecutions of unjust, powerful men, and all who are pursued or troubled by enemies.

Kyrie eleison.

Since the three-times-three petition of the Kyrie in the Roman Mass is a clear reference to the Holy Trinity, we may fittingly choose similar petitions to the Trinity from the Ethiopic Liturgy as our concluding prayer to this meditation:

*Prayer: Holy Lord God! Holy Strong One! Holy Immortal One! Have mercy on us....*

*O Holy Trinity.... Holy Unity of Nature, protect our assembled community through the merits of your saintly apostles and bring peace to us through your merciful love....*

*Sacred Trinity, have pity on us; Blessed Trinity, spare us; Holy Trinity, have compassion on us.*

# 8.

## GLORY TO GOD

GLORY TO GOD IN THE HIGHEST, AND ON EARTH PEACE TO MEN OF
GOOD WILL. WE PRAISE YOU, WE BLESS YOU, WE ADORE YOU, WE GLORIFY
YOU.

*And suddenly there was with the angel a multitude of the
heavenly host praising God and saying: Glory to God in the
highest, and on earth peace among men of good will.*

*And when the angels had departed from them into heaven, the
shepherds were saying to one another: Let us go over to Bethlehem
and see this thing that has come to pass, which the Lord has made
known to us. (Luke 2:13-15)*

This, the first great hymn of the Mass which is given specifically
to praise, is the Christian manifesto: Glory to God in the highest.
No true Christian ever considers anything higher, nor will he
accept either excuse or substitute. Glory to God above all else;
glory to God first of all, because there is no one and nothing else
higher; glory to God with the best and greatest and most perfect
of all man's gifts. The best must at all times be given to God. How
fitting that this first and most important rule of Christian life was
openly announced on the very night that the Son of God came
into this world to begin his work of redemption. How fitting that
it should be sung again at every Mass!

Christ's whole life was a glory to God, the highest glory ever given. No substitutes, no corruption of that purpose for him. Glory to God alone—not to armies and conquests, despots and political machines, material prosperity and wealth. Glory to God through justice and mercy and love and self-surrender; no glory to selfish gain and comfortable security through diplomatic talk and double-dealing. History testifies that when we depart from the glory of God, when we substitute the glory of man, we soon serve the glory of a single man, the most clever and powerful who often becomes the ruthless dictator. We who sought not God became the slaves of man. Such is the grim justice of corrupted nature; we were saved from her destruction only by the merciful intervention of God—and it must be a continuous intervention!

"Glory to God in the highest, and on earth peace to men of good will." This is the only formula for peace, order, and justice that has ever worked. How long ago and how often since has this true pattern for peace been announced to the world! Now, after two thousand years, there is no peace, no order, no justice, because the pattern has not been heeded. God never speaks in vain. "He gave them a law to follow," says the Scripture. If man does not listen, he must pay the price.

The Gloria of the Mass is filled with the praise of God. "We praise you, we speak well of you, we fall down in worship of you, we give all glory to you." Every man praises, blesses, adores, and glorifies something. We cannot live without due reverence toward our goal in life; we must follow the pattern of the Gloria, either to a true or a false end. The question is, are we idolaters or true worshippers? That is the only pertinent question; for as surely as we live, we are worshipping somewhere, at some shrine. It may be at the raw shrine of material luxury—money, fine clothes, a flashy, comfortable car, a sumptuous house (usually not much of a home), popularity and power—or at the deceptive shrine of self. Yes, we may be so blindly proud as to adore only ourselves, but even then we seek some external object in which to adore ourselves, as in a mirror. In our visions of self-grandeur we adore the crowds that we imagine are venerating us. It matters little what false temple we have worshipped in; the error is tragic and the pain of frustration is sure to come.

The Gloria of the Mass is the Christian way, the vital rule to peace and happiness. If we are to reach a true goal instead of a hopeless mirage, if all things are to be in order, if happiness and peace are to grow in our minds and hearts, we possess the only true recipe: "Glory to God in the highest." It is the one true purpose of life, and throughout the Mass we are gently, gradually, and insistently led on to this true purpose.

"Everything must crumble that is not grounded on the cornerstone which is Christ Jesus," wrote Pope Pius XI on the feast of Christ the King, in the hope that we might be saved from the evils of secularism and materialism. It is an echo of the solid conviction and direction of the Gloria of the Mass.

*Prayer: Glory be to God on high from eternal age to eternal age, world without end, and on the earth let there be peace and godly hope to men. May we be found worthy to glorify and to praise the Most High One, to give thanks and all honor to Him who lowered himself and exalted the humble Maiden; to God who made himself man and rescued men; to the Most High One who humbled himself and raised up the humiliated ones; to God who is above all things. To him be all praise and honor at this moment and on all festival days and at every instant of life, from eternity to eternity, throughout the universe without end. Amen.*

(*Preparation Prayers, Maronite Liturgy*)

# 8,b.

## WE THANK YOU

WE THANK YOU FOR YOUR GREAT GLORY, LORD GOD, HEAVENLY KING, GOD, ALMIGHTY FATHER. O LORD JESUS CHRIST, ONLY-BEGOTTEN SON, LORD GOD, LAMB OF GOD, THE FATHER'S SON, WHO TAKES THE WORLD'S SINS AWAY, HAVE MERCY ON US; WHO TAKES AWAY THE SINS OF THE WORLD, RECEIVE OUR PRAYER; WHO SITS AT THE FATHER'S RIGHT HAND, HAVE MERCY ON US.

*I give thanks to my God in all my remembrance of you, always in all my prayers making supplications for you all with joy, because of your association with me in spreading the gospel of Christ from the first day until now. (Phillipians 1:3–6)*

*We give thanks to the God and Father of our Lord Jesus Christ . . . who has made us worthy to share the lot of the saints in light. He has rescued us from the power of darkness and transferred us into the kingdom of his beloved Son, in whom we have our redemption, the remission of our sins. (Colossians 1:3, 12–14)*

The Gloria is a great chorus of praise to the one true God. But it does not forget the great mystery of heaven: God is not alone. He is mysteriously a family. He is three distinct Divine Persons, while he is yet one in a more intimate unity than any oneness we find on earth.

Our attention is first turned toward the Father, the Creator of

27

the universe, the Author of all we call glorious and beautiful. In all
his majesty, in his infinite wisdom, in the infinite distance between
his awesome divinity and our wretched humanity, he reveals himself
as our Father.

He could not do more to exalt us, to give us glory and position,
than to call himself our Father! A Father's importance reflects on
his children: the greater the father's dignity, the greater his son's.
St. John appreciated the honor we received with our position:
"Behold what charity the Father has had toward us, that we should
be called, and indeed be, the sons of God." From him all fatherhood
on earth has descended, from him all fatherly love has its name and
its power. By his gift of divine grace, we are no longer children of
men, mere imitations of the love that is in heaven; we are his
children now, chosen by himself.

"O Lord, only begotten Son, Jesus Christ." It is the Son, second
Person of the divine family, in whom we are called the children of
God. He has built the bridge, he has—in the words of the Greek
liturgy—"carried the shame of the cross and the chains of slavery.
He has broken the bars of the iron doors, and rescued the departed
souls from suffering. He has shone upon us with the brilliance of a
new light, whereas before we sat in the shadow of death."

God from all eternity understood us fully, and loved us fully
without ever becoming a man. It was for our benefit, not for his,
that the only-begotten Son joined himself to our nature. The
ancients, Hebrews as well as pagans, never came to a clear concept
of the intimate tenderness and goodness of God. Somehow God always remained a kind of exalted guess, a veiled mystery high above
them. When pagans tried to understand him more intimately, they
fell into the error of bringing him down to themselves and clothing
him with degenerate legends that soon lost meaning.

But here and now, in the reign of this emperor, Caesar Augustus,
and this tetrarch, Herod; of this mother, Mary of Nazareth; in this
place, a cave on the hill-side of Bethlehem, man could come and see
the reality. He could watch the child grow and wax strong, full of

grace with God and man; he could hear the Son of God say, "As the Father has loved me, so I have loved you."

*Prayer: Lord of all, we praise you; Christ Jesus, we glorify you, for you have given life to our bodies and by your holiness you have redeemed our souls. . . . Truly, Lord, you are the giver of life to our bodies and the most sacred redeemer of our souls and the ever-faithful protector of our earthly way. It is fitting that we should thank you, bow down before you, and give glory to you, Lord of all, Father, Son, and Holy Spirit for all eternity. Amen. Let your voices be raised, people of God, and offer praise to the God of the living. Holy God, blessed Strong One, holy Immortal One, grant us your mercy.*

**(Prayer before the Epistle, Liturgy of Malabar)**

# 8,c.

## THE ONLY HOLY ONE

For you are the only Holy One. You alone are the Lord. You only are Most High, Jesus Christ, with the Holy Spirit in the glory of God the Father. Amen.

*And they do not rest day and night, saying, Holy, holy, holy, the Lord God almighty, who was, and who is, and who is coming. And when those living creatures give glory and honor and benediction to him who sits on the throne, who lives forever and ever, the twenty-four elders will fall down before him who sits upon the throne, and will worship him who lives forever and ever, and will cast their crowns before the throne, saying, Worthy art thou, O Lord our God, to receive glory and honor and power; for thou hast created all things, and because of thy will they existed, and were created. (Apocalypse 4:8–11)*

If we try to imagine what the *Gloria in Excelsis* must be in heaven, the eternal, joyous chorus of praise, we must rely on figures and poetry, we are fully aware that we can only suggest such glory in images and symbols. In this attempt we are aided by the Apocalypse of St. John, who in a splendid series of visions saw the great trumpets, the sacred elders, the millions of resplendent martyrs, the full-winged angels and all the flaming glories of heaven surrounding a magnificent altar, on which he saw the glorified Lamb of God. Then he heard the tremendous harmonies of a new song:

> Worthy art thou to take the scroll and to open its seals;
> For thou wast slain, and hast redeemed us for God
>     with thy blood,
> Out of every tribe and tongue and people and nation,
> And hast made them for our God a kingdom and priests,
> And they shall reign over the earth.          (Apoc. 5:9–10)

This triumphant song, like the *Gloria* itself, is remarkably suited to all the great feasts of the Church year. It is a victorious Easter song in praise of the Paschal Lamb whose bloody sacrifice purchased our redemption and our resurrection. It is a song of love for the feasts of Corpus Christi and Holy Thursday, for it sings of the kingdom of God and his priesthood, found throughout the world. It is the sorrowful but confident song of Good Friday, a hymn of reverence for the Lamb that was slain on Calvary to redeem us. And it is the heavenly hymn of Christmas itself, for it accompanies a vision "filled with a multitude of angels, standing on every side of the throne, in thousands of thousands," praising the divine redeemer who became man for all men.

Nowhere in the universe is the Gloria sung as it is by the saints who have been born again in Christ, the heavenly choir that has found everlasting joy and peace in him. Yet some measure of joy is promised us on earth, too. "Peace on earth to men of good will." By that reassuring announcement we were given the privilege of joining the jubilation of heaven. So in the glorious hymn of praise, the *Gloria,* the Church rises humbly from the earth and comes forward to meet the triumphant chorus of heaven with her faint, earthly echoes: "You alone are the Holy One; you are the only Lord." She knows that her praise is feeble; she is embarrassed at the contrast between the greatest joys of this world and the joy of heaven. She knows, like the psalmist, that "His lightnings illumine the world; the earth sees and trembles. The mountains melt like wax before the Lord, before the Lord of all the earth" (Psalm 96).

Earth trembles at its own shame, earth trembles at its nothingness before the infinite beauty and goodness of God, earth trembles at the sight of man's blindness in choosing any of her treasures in preference to her Creator. "All who worship graven images are put to shame, who glory in the things of nought; all gods are prostrate before him . . . because you, O Lord, are the Most High over all the earth, exalted far above all gods" (Psalm 96). Your coming on Christmas, all the beauty of your humanity, all the perfection of your life, the tremendous gift of yourself on the Cross, the immeasurable radiance of your Resurrection—all this was but a flash of lightning, a brief instant of revelation. It exceeds all else the earth has ever known or discovered or suspected, but yet it was only a blinding flash. Our vision of your glory, Lord, is yet to come. We have seen so much, and it is all but one glimpse. The Mass expresses our desire for the full revelation and looks forward to it with confidence.

*Prayer: We send up our thanks to you, invisible King, who in your infinite power designed all things. In the fullness of your charity you caused all creation to come from nothing into being. O Heavenly Ruler, turn your eyes to those who worship you; they are not bowing their heads before flesh and blood, but before you, the all-holy God. Master, of all your gifts give us what shall benefit us according to our various needs. Sail with the seafarers, cross the land with travelers, grant healing to the sick, divine physician of both souls and bodies. Through your only-begotten Son's grace and mercy and charity for man. With him and with your ever-blessed, gracious Spirit, who gives life, you are praised now and for all eternity, from age to age. Amen.*

(*Prayer after the Opening of Doors, Byzantine Liturgy*)

# 9.

## *DOMINUS VOBISCUM*

THE LORD BE WITH YOU. AND WITH YOUR SPIRIT.

*This is how you shall bless the Israelites. Say to them: The Lord bless you and keep you! The Lord let his face shine upon you, and be gracious to you! The Lord look upon you kindly and give you peace! (Numbers 6:23-26)*

*Booz himself came from Bethlehem and said to the harvesters, 'The Lord be with you!' and they replied, 'The Lord bless you!' (Ruth 2:4)*

Eight times during the Mass, we are greeted by the words, "Dominus vobiscum," and we answer courteously, "Et cum spiritu tuo." The Lord be with you—and with your spirit, also.

This greeting is the Catholic feast-day wish for the whole year, the "Merry Christmas" and "Happy New Year" and "Congratulations" and "Happy Birthday" and all best greetings rolled into one. For what greater blessing could you wish on your family, friends, or neighbors than this: "The Lord be with you"? The Lord be with you throughout this year, and all will be well, even though you fail by the standards of this world, even though you are poor or weak or suffering, indeed, even though you die. "The Lord be with you," and all is well.

"Dominus vobiscum." It is the most courteous of greetings, finer than the most gentlemanly "How do you do" or the most charming "Good morning," more truthfully friendly than the cheeriest "hello" or "howdy" of the informal West; more intimate and sincere than the best "Glad to see you here."

"The Lord be with you." Saying this, we recognize God's image in our neighbor, God's friendship, God's love for him; we acknowledge, in fact, God's life, his grace, in our fellowman. It is the noble greeting with which the members of God's family salute each other.

"Et cum spiritu tuo." An equally generous response; the beauty of man is in his spirit: his knowledge and love, his most precious desires and feelings, his greatest hopes and his immortality; his true claim to recognition and respect are in his spirit. "The Lord be with you: and with your spirit." It is a blessing, too, similar to the benediction God prescribed in the Old Testament as a way for the priests to bless the people in his Name (quoted above).

It is a truly godly greeting and a blessing, but it is also a preparation for prayer. And that is how the Church uses this salutation in the Mass. Unless God is with us, and in our spirit, there is no real prayer. We must "sink into God," so to speak, before we will know what to say and what to think, before we are aware of his presence.

What to say: before the priest dares ascend the altar, before he so much as asks God to "take away our iniquities" that we may be worthy to enter here, to bow before this "holy of holies," he says to us: "The Lord be with you," and remembering that he, too, is but a man, we answer, "And with your spirit." Before the collected prayer of the Mass, in which our requests for the day are made, we repeat this wish.

What to think: before the Gospel is read to us, before the bread and wine are offered for us, we must be prepard to think. Before Christ can teach us, before his good news, the Gospel, can remake us, the Lord must be with us. Before we are prepared to offer ourselves, heart and soul, with Christ in his perfect sacrifice, the Lord must be with us. "The Lord be in my heart and on my lips," we say before the Gospel. We cannot think fruitfully, we cannot learn deeply, we cannot speak wisely, unless the Lord be with us.

*Prayer: Lord our God, save your people and bless your heirs; preserve in peace the full measure of your Holy Church; fill with holiness those who love the beauty of your house; make them glorious in your divine strength; and do not forsake those who place their trust in you. Lord, have compassion on us and bless us. Make the glory of your face shine upon us.*

(*Prayer of the Second Antiphon, Byzantine Liturgy*)

# 10.

## TO WHOM AM I SPEAKING?

(BEGINNING OF THE PEOPLE'S PRAYER . . .)

*Now this is everlasting life, that they may know thee, the only true God, and him whom thou has sent, Jesus Christ. (John 17:3)*
*I say to you further, that if two of you shall agree on earth about anything at all for which they ask, it shall be done for them by my Father in heaven. For where two or three are gathered together for my sake, there am I in the midst of them. (Matt. 18:19-20)*

The second part proper to each feast at the Mass is the "Collected Prayer" of those present. The title "Collect" has little meaning to the modern reader, unless he is familiar with its origin. I have chosen to call this the "People's Prayer." It is the expression of the united requests of the assembled congregation. Some missals call it the "Prayer of the Assembly" or simply "The Prayer" or the "Oration." It is a special prayer suited to the feast or season being celebrated, and gathers in itself the best of the congregation's Christian aspirations and petitions. The Church has composed these prayers for her children's instruction and benefit. Guided by the Holy Spirit, she teaches us what we ought to be asking for, an important matter in which we so often fail. St. Paul observed this weakness in man, and assured us that "the Spirit helps our weakness. For we do not know what we should pray for as we ought,

*36*

but the Spirit himself pleads for us with unutterable groanings"
(Romans 8:26).

To pray as we ought, we must first recall carefully to whom we
are speaking. If it is embarrassing for us to speak to a stranger at a
gathering without knowing his name or occupation, if we are
disappointed in not having been introduced to him, how much more
ashamed and embarrassed ought we be to talk to God without a
respectful introduction.

That is why the People's Prayer of the Mass nearly always begins
with "an introduction to God." We must know what great royal
personage we are addressing. It would be most unwise to forget it,
and a sign of true love and appreciation to spend some time preparing our weak minds for this most exalted conversation. If every
good conversationalist pays respectful attention to the person with
whom he speaks—a man he can see—how much more should we
prepare to give utmost attention to God, whom we do not see, and
who is indeed above our intellectual vision as well! "Almighty,
eternal God," the Church prays. "God, who has given to mankind
the prize of eternal salvation." "God, who appointed your only-
begotten Son to be the Savior of all men." "Almighty, ever-living
God, you who govern all things in heaven and on earth." "O God,
you know the weakness of our flesh." "God, who through your
transcendent sacraments have given new life to the world." "Lord
Jesus Christ, who in the days of your obedience to Mary and Joseph
hallowed the home life with virtues beyond telling. . . ." These are
only a few examples of how we are introduced to God in the "collected prayers" of the faithful, the formal opening prayers of the
people at Mass. We are taught much about God in these various
introductions. Sometimes the infinite goodness of the Lord is
presented to us; at other times his boundless power or his unfailing
justice or his awesome holiness or his indulgent mercy are recalled.
Often his gracious qualities are contrasted with our weaknesses, our
sins, our blindness, our helplessness. In every case, if we pay these
introductions the attention they deserve, we shall be able to pray
with far greater intelligence and love.

*Prayer: We confess your supreme excellence, Lord God, Lover of men; we lay open our weaknesses before you, and we ask you to clothe us with your strength. Forgive us our former sins, and make us into new men. Make us in fact and in deed your true servants. . . . We beg your assistance for all the faithful, for those who have come to know our Lord Jesus Christ: may their faith and wisdom and learning ever grow stronger.*

*We ask your grace for this congregation: may every member experience your mercy; give them knowledge of yourself, give them appreciation of your glory. Let them all come to know you more and more, eternal Father, and your one Son, Jesus Christ.*

*(Prayer for the People, from a Fourth Century Christian Liturgy)*

# II.

## THE REQUEST

*. . . You do not have because you do not ask. You ask and do not receive, because you ask amiss, that you may spend it upon your passions. . . . Do you not know that the friendship of this world is enmity with God? . . . Draw near to God, and he will draw near to you.* (James 4:2 *ff.*)

*And the confidence that we have towards him is this, that if we ask anything according to his will, he hears us.* (I John 5:14–15)

Because of our darkened minds and weakened hearts, the prayers of the assembled Church have a twofold purpose: to teach us how to pray, and then to express our public praise and petitions. The "Collected Prayer" is the group request of the Christian community to God through Christ. But, alas! How weak and wordly we, the Christian community, find ourselves as we begin our prayer!

Surely one thought above all strikes us as we look at each day's oration in the missal: our desires and our personal petitions are much inferior to those of the Church. Why? Because our lives are so far from Christian, so far from resembling Christ's. His single-minded attachment to his Father's plan, his overpowering devotion to the Father's will and to our redemption, his complete self-forgetfulness seem entirely out of our reach. Yet that is the goal for which we must constantly reach out; his thoughts must become our thoughts, his desires our desires. Such is the necessary purification our minds must undergo before our arrival in heaven. St. Paul's urgent insistence that we "put on the mind of Christ" is with good reason!

At private prayer how introverted and narrow our requests! What petitions are the ones that most often come to our minds when we take out a moment to pray? What small, immediate, materialistic wishes are needed to prompt us to pray earnestly! How shallow and blind our requests, how childish our demands. "We do not know what to pray for," was the penetrating observation of St. Paul. It is to our advantage a hundredfold that "the Spirit himself prays for us." And one way in which he does this is in the official prayers of the Church.

The Church pleads for us, as a mother who understands far more than do her children. "Grant us an increase of faith, hope, and charity. . . ." How sincerely do we desire those highest gifts? "Grant that we may keep our minds fixed on the things of heaven. . . ." How well are we succeeding—or rather, how much effort do we give it? "Keep us from all things harmful and lead us to all things profitable to our salvation. . . ." Quite a mouthful, that request. "Grant that we, by that same Holy Spirit, may have a right judgment in all things. . . ." Are we cooperating with the Holy Spirit on that worthy desire? "Grant that we may see Your Son without dread when he comes as our judge. . . ." A request of God that makes a few demands of us!

In the petitions of the People's Prayer, it is the Church's constant concern to bring us out of our narrow self-interest into the light of God's abundance, to make us aware of the spiritual needs of our neighbor, to make us live for our eternal goal in heaven, to make us understand those higher spiritual goods which should be our chief interest in life, to bring us in each Mass closer to God and consequently closer to our true selves. It is well worth our time to pay particular attention to these prayers!

*Prayer: We pray to the Lord for the peace and salvation of the whole world; we pray for the faithful of Christ everywhere, for those who are suffering or sorrowing or undergoing trials, for our parents and our friends and all whose duty is to govern; we pray for all the faithful who have passed into eternity before us; we beg pardon for the sins and frailties and negligences of all of us. O Lord, merciful God, lover of all men, give us grace to stand before you with devoted attention and holy fear, that we may serve you with an upright conscience and praise you as Master and Creator of all.*

(*Prayers before the Epistle, Maronite Liturgy*)

# 12.

## THROUGH JESUS CHRIST

THROUGH OUR LORD JESUS CHRIST YOUR SON, WHO LIVES AND REIGNS WITH YOU, IN UNION WITH THE HOLY SPIRIT, GOD FOREVER AND EVER. AMEN.

*And whatever you ask in my name, that I will do, in order that the Father may be glorified in the Son. (John 14:13)*

*In the name of Jesus Christ of Nazareth, whom you crucified . . . does he stand here before you, sound. . . . For there is no other name under heaven given to men by which we must be saved. (Acts 4:10, 12)*

Every prayer of the Church, particularly at the Mass, makes reference to the Holy Trinity, and is usually offered explicitly "through Jesus Christ our Lord." There are very good reasons for this, and to pray well at Mass—and to understand the Mass at all— we must have these reasons in mind.

At the last supper Jesus said to his apostles, "If you ask the Father anything in my name, he will give it to you." He told them, "You have not chosen me, but I have chosen you, and have appointed you that you should go and bear fruit, and that your fruit should remain; that whatever you ask the Father in my name he may give you" (John 15:16). And so, first of all, the Church in her form of prayer remembers the command and the promise of Christ.

Since Jesus is the true mediator between God and men, being himself both God and man, it is most fitting that on our way to God all our good works are done through him, as St. Paul advises: "Whatever you do in word or in work, do all in the name of the Lord Jesus, giving thanks to God the Father through him" (Col. 3:17).

Jesus became the mediator by uniting the family of God with the family of man. "This is my beloved Son, in whom I am well pleased," said the Father at Christ's baptism and on Mount Tabor when Jesus was glorified before his apostles. "As the Father has loved me, I also have loved you. Abide in my love. . . . In that day you shall ask in my name; and I do not say to you that I will ask the Father for you, for the Father himself loves you because you have loved me, and have believed that I came forth from God" (John 15:9, 16:27). The Father is pleased with us, too, because we are members of Christ, and lovers of Christ. If the Mass is in one sense a sacrifice of fear and trembling, sacred and precious above our understanding, it is also a family feast, a time of intimacy with God through Jesus Christ, whose members we have become through baptism.

Rejoicing over this intimacy of God with us through Jesus, St. Thomas Aquinas exclaims, in reference to the Eucharist, "There is not now and there has never been a people whose gods were as near to them as our Lord, our God, is near to us. He so wished to give us a share of his divinity that God's only-begotten Son joined himself to our human nature. And since he became man, he could make men into gods."

The apostles assure us that in God-made-man, Jesus Christ, we have become sons of God, and the Mass has become the banquet-hall and the feast of the divine family. "Behold what manner of love the Father has bestowed upon us," writes St. John the Evangelist, "that we should be called children of God; and such we are. This is why the world does not know us, because it did

not know him. Beloved, now we are the children of God, and it
has not yet appeared what we shall be. We know that, when he
appears, we shall be like to him, for we shall see him just as he is.
And every one who has this hope in him makes himself holy, just
as He also is holy" (I John 3:1-3).

*Prayer: O Father in heaven, you have given up your Son to
death to pay ransom for our sins; we beseech you, by the power of
the blood he shed, to have compassion on us, your creatures endowed
with human minds. We offer this in memory of him, your only
Son, who in his human flesh went down into the valley of death,
crashed the gates of hell, and showed us that you are the only true
God, the God of all the living and all the dead. In obedience to his
word, then, we offer you this saving mystery of your Son's Body
and Blood, while we reflect on his redemptive sufferings for us, his
crucifixion that brought us life, his victorious resurrection from the
dead, his divine and joyous ascension to heaven, to the right hand
of your throne, our Father. And we praise and await his second
glorious coming. Amen.*

*(At the Elevation, Armenian Liturgy)*

# 13.

## GOD SPEAKS TO US

(THE EPISTLE: READINGS FROM THE HOLY SCRIPTURES. . .)

*God, who at sundry times and in divers manners spoke in times past to the fathers by the prophets, last of all in these days has spoken to us by his Son, whom he appointed heir of all things, by whom also he made the world. . . .*

*Therefore ought we the more earnestly to observe the things that we have heard, lest perhaps we drift away. For if the word spoken by angels proved to be valid. . . how shall we escape if we neglect so great a salvation? For it was first announced by the Lord and was confirmed unto us by those who heard him. . . . (Hebrews 1:1, 2:1 ff.)*

The Mass is a conversation and an exchange of gifts between God and his people. The Church directs us to open the conversation, for it is we, creatures of this world, who must of our own free will prepare ourselves for this sacred exchange. God on his part is always ready and always attentive to us.

Thus the first part of the Mass has been an upward movement: its intention is to lift us, earth-bound sinners, to a quiet place where we might listen to God. In the course of our preparation, from the opening prayers to the Collect (People's Prayer), we have reminded ourselves of the four purposes of the Mass. We are to atone for our sins and weaknesses: we have begged God to accept this atonement in the *Confiteor* and the *Kyrie*. We are to praise and adore our Creator and Redeemer: we have sung a hymn of praise and thanksgiving in the *Gloria*. We have expressed adoration and gratitude. And now our petitions have also ascended to God in the Collect, the assembled petition of the people.

The second movement of the Mass is downward: it is time for God to speak to us. For this part the Church naturally turns to the inspired word of God, words specifically written under divine inspiration for our instruction. These readings from the Scripture were found in the earliest liturgies. Quite naturally, before the compilation of the completed canon of Sacred Scripture, these "lessons" varied according to the choice of individual churches, and were often ingeniously selected to fit the celebration of a local martyr-saint. The organization of the season of Lent in the fourth century led to the gradual adoption of a fixed series of appropriate lessons at the celebration of the Eucharist.

Today this second movement of the Mass consists of three parts: the Lesson, taken from an Old Testament book or a letter of the Apostles; the Gospel, proclaiming more directly the teachings of our Lord; and the Sermon, which develops further the teachings contained either in the readings, the liturgical season or the feast of the day, or in a wider sense the needs of the time.

The Lesson (Epistle) represents allegorically the preaching of the prophets (including St. John the Baptist) in preparation for the perfect fulfillment, the preaching of Christ himself as given us in the Gospel. Both parts bring us, in day-to-day and week-to-week selections, the eternally true and essential message of God. It is for us to listen, consider, meditate, and put into practice. Like the holy men of the Old Testament, our attitude must be: "Speak, Lord, your servant is listening."

*Prayer: We are mindful of our Lord, God and Redeemer Jesus Christ, and all he has done for our salvation. . . . We remember it by this Holy Eucharist on the altar before us: and we recall our father Adam and our mother Eve, Mary the holy mother of God; we recall the prophets, apostles, evangelists, preachers; we remember the martyrs, confessors and virtuous men and women of the faith, the priests, the holy teachers and true shepherds, monks and hermits, all the faithful who are with us in prayer; and with these we recall all people who have been pleasing to You, Lord, at all times past from Adam and Eve down to this day. We also remember our forefathers, our brethren, all who have brought us the message of truth, our beloved dead and all the departed faithful; we recall especially our neighbors, those who have been with us in this holy place in the past and those who are with us now, and all who are united with us in charity.*

*(Opening Prayers, Syrian Liturgy)*

# 14.

## LESSONS TO BE LEARNED

(READING OF THE WORD OF GOD: FIRST LESSON. . .)

*If you abide in my word, you shall be my disciples indeed, and you shall know the truth, and the truth shall make you free. (John 8:31)*

*Brethren, children of the race of Abraham, and all among you who fear God, to you the word of this salvation has been sent. (Acts 13:26)*

*Casting aside all uncleanness and abundance of malice, with meekness receive the ingrafted word, which is able to save your souls. (James 1:21)*

In most of the Eastern liturgies, the first part of the Eucharistic rite is called "The Liturgy of the Learners." Our whole life is a vast school, under the direction of God, but because of our darkened minds, we would learn little of its full meaning, were it not for hearing the word of God himself.

The Mass draws constantly on the word of God, the Bible, for its prayer and meditation and song. If we are to make true progress of mind and heart, we need to be soaked constantly in the word of God. We need to learn over and over that the Holy Scripture and the Church are the continuing action of God in the world. The Church by her liberal use of the word of God extends it into each day of our life, the life of each Christian community and each individual.

By her arrangement and development of Mass themes through the Entrance Song, Prayer of the People, First Lesson, Gradual and Alleluia, Gospel and Sermon, the Church makes clear to us how God's message of salvation daily enters our life and centers it, living this very day as surely as it has through recorded history. It is important that we *listen* frequently to the word of God; it is addressed to us and demands a *hearing,* a public, communal hearing, not just private meditation.

The word of God is solidly the foundation of the Church's prayer and worship. The Bible and the Missal build up each other into the unified, perfect teacher of the people of God. The Bible, which is the word of God, is presented to us in a living, day-by-day instruction through the Missal. The sacrifice of the Mass itself is the effect of the word of God, specifically of Christ in the New Testament, but just as well of the many messages of God in the Old Testament regarding a perfect and pleasing sacrifice of praise. On the other hand, the Church has depended on the Holy Scripture as a perfect guide to the prayers and thoughts she ought to have at this most solemn sacrifice.

The lessons of the Mass are fittingly called in some Missals "The Celebration of the Word." God's living word deserves the best in public praise, in community and individual attention and application; for that it was intended. In the Mass our salvation history is proclaimed to us, our redemption is outlined, we accept it, we pray and meditate on it, and then we take an active part in it through the sacrifice of Christ for us.

The readings of Holy Scripture at Mass, then, are more than historical relics; they are the application of the saving word of God to our souls and our community and in a sense to all creation around us. The lessons of the Mass make us aware, too, that the word of God necessarily lives in the Church; if it did not, she could not be the Church; she would not really be speaking for God.

The lessons assure us that now, as always before us, God is

teaching his people; he is directing them ever patiently and gently, through punishment as well as reward, through good and evil, through joy and suffering, through man's foolishness and his divine wisdom. "All Scripture has been written for our correction," writes St. Paul. The past teaches us, the sacred writers interpret it for us, the Church at Mass presents it to us—it is our privilege to listen and learn and live by it.

*Prayer: Blessed be God, the Lord and Ruler of all things, who has enlightened us by his holy wisdom. Forever let his mercy rest upon the reader and upon his listeners.*

*Shed light into the dim recesses of our understanding, Lord God of us all, to fill us with the divine word of your ordinances which bring us life. Permit us, in your clemency, to reap the fruits of the word—love, hope, health of body and salvation of spirit, and the grace to celebrate your glory in faith and constancy forever, Lord and Ruler over all, Father, Son, and Holy Spirit. Amen.*

*(Prayers for the Readings, Chaldean Liturgy)*

# 15.

## EXPRESSION OF GRATITUDE

THANKS BE TO GOD.

*Thanks be to God who has given us the victory through Our Lord Jesus Christ. (I Cor. 15:57)*

*Thanks be to God who always leads us in triumph in Christ Jesus, manifesting through us the odor of his knowledge in every place. (II Cor. 2:14)*

*Thanks be to God that you who were the slaves of sin have now obeyed from the heart that form of doctrine into which you have been delivered, and having been set free from sin, you have become the slaves of justice. (Romans 6:17)*

The first lesson has been read to us; let us hope we have learned from it. It is altogether fitting that we say, "Thanks be to God." The words should be far more than a polite, acceptable response. Too much of our life is spent saying "thank you" because it's the proper thing to do, rather than because it represents a deeply felt state of mind.

In dealing with God we gain nothing by mere formality and propriety. From the very beginning it is we, not God, who suffer from our lack of gratitude. When Jesus expressed sorrow at the ingratitude of the nine lepers, he was not really feeling sorry for himself, but for them. It was their loss that distressed him; they had missed the greater happiness of the one grateful Samaritan. The true blessing of a miracle is the joyous, grateful heart of the receiver, the increased love and appreciation of the witnesses to the miracle; this greater grace the other nine had rejected. The physical wonder was intended to produce spiritual joy.

"Thanks be to God," the Church directs us to say frequently in the Mass. We sang it in the Gloria, we say it at the close of each lesson, we will sing it at the introduction of the most sacred part of the Mass: ". . .we should always and everywhere give thanks to you, holy Lord, almighty Father. . ." (Preface). The whole Mass is a thanksgiving offering; the sense of gratitude and appreciation pervades its every prayer. Twice at the end of the Mass we repeat that prayer, "Thanks be to God," and we ought to understand why.

One of the reasons for which Christ gave us the Mass, "the bread of the Eucharist," is, according to St. Justin the Martyr, "that through it we would give thanks to God for creating the world and everything in it for the sake of man." Origen adds that if we are at all true Christians, "we are by no means men with ungrateful hearts." He writes, "We are ashamed not to be thankful to God, who pours out benefits for us. The token of our thanksgiving to God is the Bread which we call the Eucharist."

*Prayer: Give thanks to the Lord, for he is good, for his mercy endures forever; give thanks to the God of gods, for his mercy endures forever; give thanks to the Lord of lords, for his mercy endures forever; who alone does great wonders. . . , who made the heavens in wisdom. . . , who remembered us in our abjection. . . and freed us from our foes. . . , who gives food to all flesh, for his mercy endures forever. Give thanks to the God of heaven, for his mercy endures forever.*

*(From Psalm 135)*

# 16.

## GRADUAL ENLIGHTENMENT

THIS IS THE DAY WHICH THE LORD HAS MADE; BE GLAD AND REJOICE IN IT. GIVE PRAISE TO THE LORD, FOR HE IS GENEROUS; HIS MERCY REMAINS FOREVER. ALLELUIA, ALLELUIA. CHRIST OUR PASCHAL VICTIM IS SACRIFICED. (GRADUAL AND ALLELUIA OF EASTER)

*I remember the deeds of the Lord; yes, I remember your wonders of old. And I meditate on your works; your exploits I ponder. O God, your way is holy; what great god is there like our God? You are the God who works wonders; among the peoples you have made known your power. (Psalm 76:13-15)*

The Gradual or Tract or Alleluia Verses are brief reflections or meditations on the reading just completed (the Epistle) and the reading about to begin (the Gospel). It is a kind of miniature dialogue; God speaks to us in the Scripture readings; we answer thoughtfully and prayerfully. Most of the Graduals and Tracts are prayers from the psalter, chosen to fit the readings—and consequently, the feast day or season. They are songs that reflect God's word.

But we may see even more in the Gradual and Alleluia, a fuller meaning and further symbolism. All of life is a slow unfolding of mystery. And contrary to our first hopes, mystery does not become smaller or simpler, but deeper and stranger, the more it unfolds.

*53*

It is like the opening of a rose, wherein we discover more and more beauty as the hidden petals come to light.

The great mystery of life, upon which all others depend, is God's purpose in placing us here on earth at all. The unfolding of this divine plan is the theme of Holy Scripture, written under God's special guidance. These lessons of life are given us in the Epistles of the Mass. They are often taken from the Old Testament, in which God began with simple and everyday comparisons to educate his people towards true worship, moral uprightness, and fundamental charity.

We must be brought gradually to full spiritual wisdom if we are to pass into the presence of God and the complete happiness of which we are capable. This mature and complete revelation is given us in the Gospel, when we hear the kingdom of heaven described by the Son of God himself.

Approaching this full light of Christ is a *gradual* growth, step by step. That, we might say, is what the *Gradual* of the Mass represents: another step, a *gradus,* toward the central action and mystery of the Mass: the very presence of Jesus Christ on the altar, our priest, our offering, our gift, our salvation.

The Gradual of the Mass is the symbol of a stage of Christian life on earth. From a simple childhood dealing almost entirely with the everyday events in our small environment, we must pass into mature age and full understanding of our purpose in life and concern for our fellowmen everywhere in the world. The way between is difficult—the way of youth, too ripe for absolute childlike confidence and obedience, too green for wisdom and sound judgment. Such is the *gradual* of our life, the stepping stone of gradual enlightenment. That is why we beg God to give our youth the grace and the strength to find their way across the stepping place, lest it become a tripping stone.

Following the Gradual, the stepping stone between the first lesson of the Mass and the Gospel, there is an Alleluia verse, a song of praise. The Gospel is the good news of Christ's coming. If, as St. Bernard writes, the very name of Jesus is "a shout of gladness in the heart," it is no wonder that the Church introduces his words, his sacred teaching, and his holy example in the Gospel with "a shout of gladness," the Alleluia, which from ancient times has been a song of praise. The very word itself means "Praise God." Praise him, for as the Gospel informs us, our redemption is accomplished.

An example of the *gradual* step may be taken from the Mass of our Lady's Assumption. In the Epistle we have heard of the saintly Judith of the Old Testament, who because of the distress of her people risked her life to prevent their ruin, to "save them in the presence of God." The Gradual, from Psalm 44, introduces us to the "king's daughter," a mysterious lady who shall "please the king with her beauty," thus interceding for her people.

The Alleluia verse completes the message. This royal princess, "Mary . . . has been taken up into heaven," and her presence "makes the angels rejoice." Then in the Gospel we are given the completed revelation in the mouth of Elizabeth: Mary is the new and perfect Judith, because she is "the mother of my Lord . . . , blessed among women," for bringing us the Divine Savior, who once for all has rescued us from ruin.

*Prayer: Lord and Lover of all mankind, let the pure light of your heavenly wisdom kindle our hearts and penetrate the eyes of our souls, that they may perceive what you are teaching us in the Gospel. Inspire in us a reverence for your most holy commandments; thus beating down the unruly desires of the flesh, we may pursue the spiritual life, in which we see all creation illumined by your holy will, and in this light our actions will follow. For you are the shining light of both spirit and flesh, Christ our God; to you we give glory, to you and your eternal Father and your most holy and loving and life-giving Spirit, both now and for all eternity. Amen.*

(*Prayer before the Gospel, Byzantine Liturgy*)

# 17.

## WORTHY OF THE GOSPEL

Purify my heart and my lips, almighty God, as you purified the lips of Isaias the prophet with a burning coal. In your merciful kindness be pleased so to cleanse me that I may worthily announce your holy Gospel, through Christ our Lord. Amen.

The Lord be in my heart and on my lips, that I may rightly and properly proclaim his holy Gospel. Amen.

*And I [Isaias] said: Woe is me, because I have held my peace; because I am a man of unclean lips, and I dwell in the midst of a people that has unclean lips, and I have seen with my eyes the King, the Lord of hosts.*

*And one of the seraphims flew to me, and in his hand was a live coal, which he had taken with the tongs off the altar. And he touched my mouth, and said: Behold, this has touched thy lips, and thy iniquities shall be taken away, and thy sin shall be cleansed. (Isaias 6:5-7)*

*Let your lives be worthy of the Gospel of Christ; so that whether I come and see you, or remain absent, I may hear . . . that you are steadfast in one spirit, with one mind striving together for the faith of the gospel. (Philippians 1:27)*

When the Mass-book is moved from the Epistle side to the Gospel side of the altar—symbolic, we may say, of the transition from the

Old to the New Testament—we rise for the reading of the Gospel. Standing has long been a sign of reverence: we stand out of respect and good manners when an important personage enters a room. It is a sign of obedience: a soldier stands at attention awaiting his orders; we stand at attention to hear and carry out the words of Christ. It is connected with eager attention: people stand to hear or see better at a public performance. Standing is evidence of respect and love: people stand to pay tribute to a great man, to give a rousing applause to a favorite personality. We stand out of love and honor for the words and actions of Christ our Redeemer.

Nowhere is greater honor paid the Holy Scripture than in the Catholic Church, where it is used in so many ways throughout our public worship, especially in the most sacred ceremonies of the Church, those of the Mass. At solemn Mass a procession is formed for the reading of the Gospel; the celebrating priest gives a special blessing to the deacon "that he may worthily read the holy Gospel." The deacon himself has knelt and asked God to "purify his lips with a burning coal, as he was pleased to cleanse the lips of the prophet Isaias," so that he might fittingly announce the Gospel. This prayer is said by the priest himself at every Mass, bowing low to the altar before the Gospel.

All this is evidence of the Church's reverence for the words of Christ. True love has never been without a strong element of awe, sacredness and respect in it. Nothing is too good for the beloved; great care is taken to protect the dignity of the one we love.

In addition to the loving attention we show our Lord by the petition, "purify my lips," and by standing out of respect for his Gospel, there is also an element of emphasis. If any message ever announced was worthy of universal attention, if any words written ever demanded the closest scrutiny, if any book ever required serious reading and re-reading, then surely the Gospel stands first. Of all news, this is the best news. Of all directions for successful living, these are the best. Of all hope and all promises ever offered mankind, the Gospel is the greatest.

Indeed, the Church has employed a very dignified restraint in the

few, calm signs of love and respect she employs. What king or
philosopher, what genius or prophet has spoken with half the
power of Christ? Let all earth keep silent when God arises to speak,
said the psalmist. In the Gospel, God arises to speak.

"Never has man spoken as this man speaks," said the Jews. When
we listen attentively to the Gospel, we understand what they meant.

*Prayer: O Lord, our God and Rescuer, lover of human kind, you
have sent out men to pour out your holiness and announce your
charity to the ends of the earth, you have bidden them spread the
good news of your kingdom, heal the ills and the sorrows of the
people, and reveal the secret hidden through the centuries.*

*Now, Lord, our mighty King and holy God, pour out your grace
on us, send light into our minds and hearts, and fill us with the
power of wisdom to hear the words of your holy Gospel. Let us
more than listen; let us do, and bear abundant fruit, this one thirty-
fold, that one sixty-fold, and another a hundred-fold; thus will you
hear us, too, a people burdened with sin, praying for the coming
of the heavenly kingdom.*

(Prayer before the Gospel, Ethiopic Liturgy)

# 18.

## WHAT THE GOSPEL SAYS

(READING FROM THE HOLY GOSPELS.)

*I am not ashamed of the gospel, for it is the power of God unto*
*salvation to everyone who believes, to Jew first and then to Greek.*
*For in it the justice of God is revealed, from faith unto faith, as it*
*is written, He who is just lives by faith. (Romans, 1:16–17)*

*And Jesus returned in the power of the Spirit into Galilee. . . .*
*And he came to Nazareth, where he had been brought up; and*
*according to his custom, he entered the synagogue on the Sabbath*
*and stood up to read. And the volume of Isaias the prophet was*
*handed to him. And after he opened the volume, he found the place*
*where it was written: 'The Spirit of the Lord is upon me because*
*he has anointed me; to bring good news to the poor he has sent*
*me, to proclaim to the captives release, and sight to the blind; to set*
*at liberty the oppressed, to proclaim the acceptable year of the Lord,*
*and the day of recompense.' And closing the volume, he gave it back*
*to the attendant and sat down. And the eyes of all in the synagogue*
*were gazing on him. (Luke 4:14 ff.)*

It was Jesus himself who in his own reading of the prophet Isaias
(whom we might fittingly call "the fifth gospel") made clear the
power of the word of God. There on the scroll was the written word
of the Lord, and here before the eyes of the people was that word

fulfilled, brought to action, the reality they could see, the very *word made flesh*. So it is in the Mass: the word of the Gospel is read to us, the message of Christ's redemption; and then it is made real before us, the powerful, effective, creative word of God. "This is my Body," and the word is made flesh before us. God's promise is fulfilled for all time and all people; the message of salvation brings about the reality of salvation; God's word is victorious. The Gospel is "the power of God unto salvation."

We stand for the Gospel of the Mass, then, as we stand to honor a victory: a victorious conclusion to a great athletic contest, a victorious General entering an assembly hall, a national hero receiving a much-deserved award and ovation. The Gospel is a message of victory. Not only the victory of salvation on the Cross and the victory over death on Easter morning. It is the victory of life contained in every word of Christ's teaching.

What do we want most on earth, but to learn during our life the way to ultimate success and glory? The Gospel is our road to victory; the Gospel is "good news" because it has taught us how to overcome every weakness, every temptation, every deception, every obstacle that drags men to defeat.

The paradoxes of the Gospel are the final message, the fullness of God's wisdom, the dynamic word for which mankind waited. The Gospel illumined the way to happiness through sorrow, the secret of imperishable wealth through poverty, of undying love through sacrifice, of eternal pride and exaltation through humility, of invincible freedom through obedience, of saving one's life through losing it. "Unless the grain of wheat fall into the ground and die, it remains alone. But if it dies, it brings forth much fruit. . . . For he who hates his life in this world, keeps it unto life everlasting." (John 12:24)

We hear in the Gospel how the Son of God came to this world and made his all-important choice—a choice which thenceforward confronted his followers—his selection of what was most worthy of his supreme dignity: the cold and poverty at Bethlehem, the precarious journey to Egypt, the twenty-some years of silent, thankless labor as Nazareth's carpenter, the consequent rejection by neighbors, friends and enemies alike, the envy and hatred of his nation's leaders. A man misunderstood, unappreciated, slandered, condemned, despised, imprisoned, falsely accused, spat upon, scourged, tortured, left to die on a tree. The world was cleansed for all time in the pure white fire of his total sacrifice, burning bright and untarnished on the unbent wick of perfect innocence. No weakness, no helplessness, no ignorance, no blemish, no thwarting of purpose offered any excuse or explanation. The undiminished divine will and the unshadowed divine innocence had selected this way fully and deliberately; here was God's design, written straight and clear. "He emptied himself, taking the form of a slave." He chose the painful path: "He was sacrificed because He willed it." He gave the last full measure of love: "He tasted death for us all."

No higher ideal, no greater love, no fuller sacrifice, no clearer innocence, no nobler acceptance, no more generous forgiveness could ever sanctify the earth again. The good news of the Gospel is that man's highest ideal has been reached, has become an accomplished fact, has swept clean the earth, has dispelled darkness and ignorance and despair and slavery to evil forever.

*Prayer: The right hand of our Lord Jesus Christ, the strong arm of his almighty power, the invisible might of his omnipotence, bringing all benediction and all the graces of life; the power which descended on the apostles in the upper room of Sion and sanctified them on the Mount of Olives, descend upon you, my brethren, defend you and persevere with you to the end, all who read and listen....*

*Peace be to you. Glory, honor and praise to Jesus for his life-giving message, to the Father who sent him for our redemption, to the Holy Spirit, from eternity to eternity forever.*

(*Prayers before and after the Gospel, Maronite Liturgy*)

# 19.

## THE SERMON

*Go into the whole world and preach the gospel to every creature.*
*He who believes and is baptized shall be saved, but he who does*
*not believe shall be condemned. (Mark 16:15)*

*Brethren, children of the race of Abraham, and all among you*
*who fear God, to you the word of this salvation has been sent.*
*For the inhabitants of Jerusalem and its rulers, not knowing him*
*and the utterances of the prophets which are read every Sabbath,*
*fulfilled them by sentencing him; and though they found no ground*
*for putting him to death, they asked of Pilate permission to kill*
*him. And when they had carried out all that had been written*
*concerning him, they took him down from the tree and laid him*
*in a tomb. But God raised him from the dead on the third day;*
*and he was seen during many days by those who had come up with*
*him from Galilee to Jerusalem; and they are now witnesses for him*
*to the people. So we now bring you the good news that the promise*
*made to our fathers, God has fulfilled . . . in raising up Jesus.*
*(Sermon of St. Paul, Acts 13:26 ff.)*

Here is one example of how the apostles preached the message of
salvation. The sermon is essentially the conveyance of God's word
to the people, to enlighten them on its meaning, to convince them

62

of its reality, to apply its power to their daily lives—their work, their conversation, their prayer and their play, their community and their families, their attitude and their every action. From the great task confronting the preachers of God's message, we glean some realization of the power and effect such preaching must have. In most cases, the message of God read in the Propers of the Mass up to this point will not be well understood or clearly remembered or carried into daily life unless it is forcefully emphasized by the sermon. Much can be done by the preacher to fix the day's lesson in the minds of the listeners, to show them why they have come to Mass, what they are to do as their part in the sacrifice that follows, what the Mass is to mean in the day and the week that follows, what change their intimate sharing with Christ should effect in themselves and their surroundings.

But we who listen cannot be passive spectators who await entertainment, who have come merely "to listen to a speaker," or, worse yet, to criticize him or to ignore him. No part of the Mass is "performed" for us, as though it were a staged drama. It is our personal action, our own conversation with God, we speaking to him, he speaking to us; our personal gift of attention and self-sacrifice to him, his offering of himself—the Cross renewed——for our sins and our needs, his sacramental nourishment given to us. The real work of the sermon is also our own work, our own development of attitude, our growing conviction that we need to hear God's word, over and over; that we need further enlightenment on how to apply it; that we cannot hear it too often; that we must carry it everywhere with us; that we should be more concerned with what is said than how it is said or by whom it is said. St. Teresa of Avila observed how a soul can measure its own progress by its attitude towards every sermon, however poor its construction or delivery; in her own experience, she saw that only after she seriously began to meditate, firmly decided to give up certain worldly attachments, and made the effort to come ever closer to God—then, only then, did she benefit in real measure from the sermons she heard. "Now," she says in substance, "I learned far

more from poor sermons than I had from the most excellent ones
before." It takes much preparation and much labor to be a good
listener—to listen properly. This means, in effect, what St. John observed, "He who does the truth comes to the light." We must, in a
certain sense, be "doers" of the word before we can be true "hearers"
of it; a paradox that will be understood by those who have experienced spiritual progress in their own lives.

*Prayer: Praise and honor to our Lord Jesus Christ for his life-
giving words, to the Father who sent him as our Savior, and to the
Holy Spirit who gives us life in his life, for all eternity. Amen.*

*(Prayer after the Gospel, Syrian Liturgy)*

# 20.

## I BELIEVE

I BELIEVE IN ONE GOD THE ALMIGHTY FATHER, CREATOR OF HEAVEN AND EARTH, OF ALL THINGS VISIBLE AND INVISIBLE. I BELIEVE IN ONE LORD JESUS CHRIST, THE ONLY-BEGOTTEN SON OF GOD, BORN OF THE FATHER BEFORE ALL AGES OF TIME; HE IS GOD OF GOD AND LIGHT OF LIGHT AND TRUE GOD OF TRUE GOD, BEGOTTEN, NOT MADE, BEING OF ONE SUBSTANCE WITH THE FATHER, THROUGH WHOM ALL CREATION CAME TO BE. FOR US MEN AND FOR OUR SALVATION HE DESCENDED FROM HEAVEN. HE WAS MADE FLESH BY THE HOLY SPIRIT FROM THE VIRGIN MARY, AND BECAME MAN.

THEN HE WAS CRUCIFIED FOR US UNDER PONTIUS PILATE; HE SUFFERED DEATH AND WAS BURIED; HE AROSE FROM DEATH ON THE THIRD DAY, AS FORETOLD IN THE SCRIPTURES. AND HE WENT UP TO HEAVEN, TAKING HIS PLACE AT THE RIGHT HAND OF THE FATHER. HE SHALL COME THENCE WITH GLORY TO JUDGE THE LIVING AND THE DEAD; OF HIS KINGDOM THERE SHALL BE NO END. I BELIEVE IN THE HOLY SPIRIT, LORD AND GIVER OF LIFE, WHO COMES FORTH FROM THE FATHER AND THE SON; HE IS ADORED AND GLORIFIED AS ONE WITH THE FATHER AND THE SON; HE IT IS WHO SPOKE THROUGH THE PROPHETS.

I BELIEVE IN ONE, HOLY, CATHOLIC AND APOSTOLIC CHURCH;

I PROFESS ONE BAPTISM FOR THE FORGIVENESS OF SINS;

I ANTICIPATE THE RESURRECTION OF THE DEAD AND THE LIFE OF THE WORLD TO COME.

AMEN.

*Go and make disciples of all nations, baptizing them in the name of the Father, and of the Son, and of the Holy Spirit, teaching them to observe all that I have commanded you. (Matthew, 28:19)*

*He who believes and is baptized shall be saved, but he who does not believe shall be condemned. (Mark 16:16)*

*One body and one Spirit, even as you were called in one hope of your calling; one Lord, one faith, one Baptism; one God and Father of all, who is above all, and throughout all, and in us all. (Ephesians 4:4–6)*

The Creed in its origin is a profession of faith in preparation for baptism. It was used for that purpose in the early Church, and is used for it today. When we say the Nicene Creed thoughtfully, we notice how it stresses unity: "I believe in *one* God . . . and in *one* Lord Jesus Christ . . . and in *one* Catholic and Apostolic Church . . . and in *one* baptism for the forgiveness of sin."

The Creed purifies and unites our hearts through the faith we profess by it. It is an excellent conclusion to the reading service, the "celebration of the word of God." It is our joyous confession of firm belief in the message we received through the Epistle and Gospel.

It is also, in a sense, a fitting preface to the sacrifice of the Mass itself. Looking upon the Mass as the great action, the great miracle of Christ, we may recall that it was our Lord's practice on earth to require an open profession of faith before working a miracle. "Take courage, son, your faith has saved you," he said to one paralytic. "If you can have faith, all things are possible," he said to another before curing his son. "Do you believe in the Son of God?" he asked of the blind man. Our Lord required faith as a necessary preface to the great signs and wonders which he worked.

Before making his astounding and solemn promises concerning the great miracle of the Holy Eucharist, Jesus insisted that his listeners must have faith to profit by the bread of life. "Do not be concerned about the food that is bound to perish, but about the food that gives eternal life. This food the Son of Man will give you." Then when his listeners asked him just what God required of them, he answered, "This is the work of God, that you believe in the One whom he has sent." With this prefatory summons to faith, Jesus began his long discourse with the people, introducing the Bread of Life, necessary to all who wished salvation and final resurrection.

It is not hard to determine why these earthly people were doubtful about the promised miracle of the Holy Eucharist, the Son of God giving his flesh for the life of men. The words themselves were "hard to bear," they said. But the reason? They had no clear faith in the Son of God's divine power, in his mission from God the Father, and in the means by which men were to be saved. And this very faith is what we reiterate in the Creed of the Mass.

Jesus made clear this requirement of full faith in connection with the Bread of Life when he answered the doubting crowd, "Does this make you waver in your faith? What then if you should see the Son of Man ascending to where he was before? It is the spirit that gives life; the flesh profits nothing. The words that I have spoken to you are spirit and life. But there are some among you who do not believe." And finally, he added the Father's part in this sacrament of "spirit and life" by saying, "This is why I have said to you, 'No one can come to me unless he is enabled to do so by my Father.'"

Can it be that our faith, too, is weak as we approach the solemn sacrifice of his Flesh and Blood? It is time, now, to strengthen and renew it. For the bread we are about to offer, and its miraculous change into his Flesh and Blood, are indeed spirit and life, understood by faith. It is altogether fitting that we say the Creed thoughtfully, to nourish that faith.

*Prayer: (In most of the Eastern liturgies the Creed is included, either said or sung. Following is a prayer from the Ethiopic Liturgy, said after the singing of the Nicene Creed) O mighty and everlasting Lord, you created man unblemished; then through the evil temptations of Satan, death first came into the world. But you conquered death by the coming of your only-begotten Son, our Lord and God and Savior Jesus Christ, who gave life to us; thus you filled the*

*world with your divine peace. The army of angels praises you with
the words, Glory to God in the highest heaven, his peace and
benevolence are poured out upon men on earth. Lord, fill our souls
with good will, and remove from us all impurity and spite and
envy; drive out all evil deeds and all deadly designs of malice; rather
let us fittingly greet one another with a sacred kiss . . . and may we
be favored with worthiness to accept your heavenly, eternal gifts.
Through Jesus Christ our Lord; to him and to you in unity with
the Holy Spirit be power and glory for all ages. Amen.*

# 21.

## THE OFFERTORY CHANT

"Confirm, O God, what you have accomplished in us; in your temple, which is in Jerusalem, kings will bring you gifts, Alleluia." (Pentecost, Offertory. Ps. 67)

"The kings of Tharsis and the islands shall offer presents; the kings of Arabia and Saba shall bring him gifts; all kings of the earth shall adore him; all nations shall serve him." (Epiphany, Offertory. Ps. 71)

"The priests of the Lord offer incense and loaves to God, and hence to their God they shall be sacred, and shall not defile his name, Alleluia." (Corpus Christi, Offertory. Leviticus 21:6)

". . . Sacrifices and prayers we offer you, Lord; accept them in behalf of those souls whom we commemorate today; let them pass from death to life, Lord, that life you promised to Abraham and his seed." (Offertory of Requiem Mass)

*And the people rejoiced when they promised their offerings willingly, because they offered them to the Lord with all their heart; and David the king rejoiced also with a great joy.*

*I [David] know my God that thou provest hearts and lovest simplicity, wherefore I also in the simplicity of my heart have joyfully offered all these things; and I have seen with great joy thy people, who are here present, bring thee their offerings. (I Chronicles 29:9, 17)*

In the earlier liturgies of the Church as well as in many of the Eastern liturgies today, the instructional part of the Mass is concluded with a general prayer for those present and for the needs of the Church throughout the world. Sometimes it is a litany of intentions both comprehensive in its attention to all the needs of mankind and beautiful in its expression of them. Such a prayer of our spiritual and temporal thanksgivings and requests are a most fitting conclusion to the first part of the Mass, and an excellent introduction to the sacrifice we are now to offer. It may seem selfish to add numerous petitions to our offering of bread and wine, as though to ask more in return than what we offer. After all, God showers us with gifts at every moment—the gift of life, all its needs, all its powers and enjoyments—while how much do we offer in appreciation? For how many of us is this offering the best attention we give to God all week, if not nearly the *only* real attention we give him?

But our lives should not be so one-sided. The Mass is far more than our offering to God; from its very nature, we may rather assume that it is God's offering to us. We may really say this sacrifice is Jesus, the Son of God, giving himself to us, as well as it is Jesus giving himself to the Father on our behalf; indeed, it is the Father's own great gift to us: "God so loved the world that he gave his only-begotten Son to the world"—so that we would once for all have a sacrifice worthy of offering.

The children of God have always realized that they must take a real part in this offering. To accomplish this in a true sense as well as a symbolic sense, the faithful brought bread and wine of their own, to be offered to God and used for the consecration into the Body and Blood of Christ. No more sacred gifts could be brought, in view of what the bread and wine were to become. During this solemn procession of offering to the altar, various scriptural passages were sung; thus the Offertory Chants were developed. The text of these chants did not necessarily refer to the offerings themselves; but in today's proper Masses a number of chants, such as the ones introducing this meditation, do make reference to the offering of these gifts.

In the early Church the people offered large amounts of bread and wine at this time, more than was needed for the actual consecration of the Mass. The offerings were collected by deacons and placed on tables near the altar; this practice may help explain some reference to "these gifts" in the offertory prayers and other later prayers. The bread and wine not used at the Mass itself was set aside for distribution to the poor. Since the eleventh century, offerings of gold, silver, precious objects and money were made.

We should readily understand the spiritual significance of the offerings and the prayers that accompany them. A further symbol, to aid our thoughts, is used at Solemn High Mass—the offering of incense, with the meaningful prayer, "Let my prayer rise before you like incense, Lord; the lifting of my hands like an evening sacrifice." The prayer and the lifting of hands are outward expressions of the lifting of mind and heart, the purification of all our mental and emotional life by attaching them to the service of God, making them subject to the infinitely wise and perfect will of God. All that we have, all that we are or will ever be is a pure gift of God; it is clear that if we are to return his generous love, all must be offered to him in return—and this means that nothing in life is ever to become more important to us than the service of God. If we understand the meaning of the Offertory at all, we realize that nothing short of total self-surrender is demanded of us, and nothing short of total devotion is good enough.

*Prayer:*
*(Priest) Let us offer our prayers to the Lord.*
*(People) Lord, have mercy.*
*(Priest) For the sacred gifts offered here, let us offer prayer to the Lord.*
*(People) Lord, have mercy.*
*(Priest) For this holy assembly and for all who come in with*

*faith, the spirit of worship and the reverent fear of God, let us offer
prayer to the Lord.*

(*People*) *Lord, have mercy.*

(*Priest*) *For our rescue from all harm and punishment and
destitution, let us pray to the Lord.*

(*People*) *Lord, have mercy.*

(*Litany of the Offertory, Byzantine Liturgy*)

# 22.

## AN INVITATION

(THE MASS AS GOD'S INVITATION TO LOVE. . . .)

*It has been my heart's desire to eat this paschal supper with you.* (*Luke 22:15*)

*Come to me, all you who labor and are burdened, and I will refresh you.* (*Matt. 11:28*)

One of the most common signs of friendship in our time is the custom of inviting people to our home for a meal. As soon as we get to know a new acquaintance well enough to like him and call him a friend, we ask him over for coffee, for lunch, and finally, "Would you have dinner with us next Sunday?" If he appreciates our friendship, he accepts, and if he is able to return the invitation, it is very likely that he and his family will do so.

The Mass is a double invitation of this kind. God invites us and we invite him. By instituting the Mass as a banquet, and bidding his disciples to continue it "in commemoration of me," Jesus invited us first. In his name, he asked his apostles and the Church they established to perpetuate this "communion of the breaking of the bread," this banquet of love and friendship with God. That the apostles understood his invitation and gave it central importance in the infant Church we can see by their frequent reference to it.

St. Luke tells us how after Jesus' Resurrection two disciples "recognized him in the breaking of the bread," when he came in to supper with them (Luke 24:35). He says of the early Christians that they "continued steadfastly in the teaching of the apostles and in the communion of the breaking of the bread and in the prayers" (Acts 2:42). St. Paul speaks at length of worthiness in a man when he comes to eat the Lord's supper, and the reference is clearly to the Eucharistic celebration.

Jesus himself had made the invitation clear and urgent and necessary for our eternal salvation. He had fed a crowd of some fifteen thousand or more in his miracle of the loaves and fishes. As a sequel to the miracle and in connection with it, he invited all to a greater, spiritual feast. "Do not labor for the food that perishes, but for that which endures unto life everlasting, which the Son of Man will give you. For upon him the Father, God himself, has set his seal." In these words, he assured us that his invitation comes from his Father, too. And in his discourse on the Holy Eucharist, as recorded by St. John (chapter 6), he gives the invitation the utmost prominence and importance.

The Mass, then, is our seal of friendship with God through Jesus Christ. He has invited us to supper, has assured us that it is his heart's desire to have us, and has said that he wishes to invite us always: "I am the bread of life. Whoever comes to me will never hunger . . . and when anyone comes to me, I will certainly not reject him."

But we invite him, too, by first laying our gifts on the altar, and then asking him to come down and accept them and change them and be present with us sacramentally. The bread is our gift to God; with it should go the gift of ourselves, our wholehearted return invitation. Jesus Christ has invited us here; we invite him to come to us, too, in the bond of lasting friendship. We are ready and eager, now, to meet at the table of the Lord.

It follows clearly from this divine invitation what a close bond of charity and friendship with one another we ought to have; Jesus invited us in his discourse at Capharnaum, gave us the reality at the Last Supper, and then prayed to his Father that we "all may be one, as you, Father, and I are one." To assure us what love for one another this demanded, he insisted that "by this all men shall know you are my disciples, that you have love for one another."

The Mass is the one great concrete reality after which our whole life must be patterned: a constant, unchanging invitation of love. God invites us perpetually, we return the invitation continually. The Mass is clearly the earthly foretaste and pledge of the eternal banquet of heaven. How ashamed we often must be to find in our brethren outside the Catholic fold (in which the Eucharist is daily celebrated for all the people) a greater appreciation for this invitation than we have ever found in ourselves.

A true Christian is fully aware that no invitation, no friendship, no love, no feast, no joy can be half as great as that which God offers us at the holy table of his divine Son, where the bread of life is brought from heaven to man. All day long our every thought and desire and work ought to be directed toward that altar as the pledge of a boundless love in which we share—with our neighbor as well as with God—and can never lose except through our own fault; and all we do ought to be a thanksgiving for that privilege. The altar is the symbol of our very existence, the reason for which we were created.

*Prayer: Now, with confidence and faith we ask our Lord, our God and Savior Jesus Christ, to make us worthy at this time of sacrifice and prayer; may he hear the requests of our hearts and voices; may he wipe out our sins and have compassion on us. May our prayers and petitions ascend with favor before his divine majesty; may he strengthen us in unity of faith and in the integrity of good works; may the almighty Lord pour out the favor of his mercy on us and bring us his clemency and salvation.*

*(Prayer after the Creed and Profession of Faith, Armenian Liturgy)*

# 23.

## WE OFFER

HOLY FATHER, ALMIGHTY AND ETERNAL GOD, ACCEPT THIS UNBLEM-
ISHED HOST WHICH I, YOUR UNWORTHY SERVANT, OFFER TO YOU, MY
TRUE AND LIVING GOD, FOR MY OWN UNCOUNTED SINS, OFFENSES, AND
FAILINGS; I OFFER IT FOR ALL WHO ARE PRESENT HERE, AND FOR ALL
FAITHFUL CHRISTIANS, LIVING AND DEAD, THAT IT MAY BRING SAVING
STRENGTH TO THEM AND TO ME, TOWARD THE GOAL OF ETERNAL LIFE.
AMEN.

*Every high priest taken from among men is appointed for men
in the things pertaining to God, that he may offer gifts and sacrifices for sins. He is able to have compassion on the ignorant and
erring, because he himself is also beset with weakness, and by reason
thereof is obliged to offer for sins, as on behalf of the people, so also
for himself. (Hebrews 5:1-3)*

The Mass is not only an invitation to supper; it is also an exchange
of gifts. We are gathered around the table of Christ in the deepest
friendship and charity. We exchange not only kind words, but the
best of gifts—from us to God, and from God to us. For this festival
and pledge of friendship we have the example of Jesus: "This is my
Body, *given for you.* . . . This is my Blood, *shed for you and for
many,* for the remission of sins." The *offering* of himself is intimately linked with the Last Supper of Jesus. The miracle of chang-

ing the bread and wine into his Body and Blood has a purpose beyond merely amazing us and strengthening our faith. It is done in order that he may be offered for us: "given for you, shed for you."

Just as the food of the paschal meal which Jesus and his disciples ate before the consecration of the bread was also something sacred set aside for God, so is the Offertory which precedes the Consecration of every Mass. As the food at the paschal table was blessed and offered to God, so is the bread and wine at the altar. As the individual items of the paschal meal signified specific benefits that God had given to his people, so do the bread and wine, the incense and the gifts of the faithful and the washing of hands. These preparatory things are part of the Christian banquet. "While they were at supper, Jesus took bread and blessed it. . . ."

We begin this sacred banquet by making the bread our gift to God, begging him to be pleased to change it into the Body and Blood of his only-begotten Son—not surely because of our worthiness, but because of his love, which desires to give us the perfect gift to offer.

Although the Son of God will then offer himself, *we* must offer, too, if it is to be our gift. We begin the offering of our gift and ourselves by using a creation of our own hands, the bread. It is the gift we have brought; it represents us, and we join it with our minds and hearts. "The gift without the giver is bare." We hope that as the bread is changed into Christ, so we who are by attention and love united with the bread may also be changed spiritually into Christ, may put on the mind of Christ as the bread becomes Christ sacramentally, may offer ourselves in the perfect spirit of Christ and be chosen by him as the bread is chosen. Then we ourselves and our desires, our love and our way of life may become part of that worthy offering "for our own salvation and that of the whole world."

We have now truly begun the Sacrifice of the Mass. We have taken the bread and proclaimed it to be set aside for the special service of God. It is our first visible offering to him, and thereafter is destined to become an infinitely greater gift.

*Prayer: Day by day we owe praise and gratitude, worship and honor, most worthy and boundless esteem to Jesus Christ, the high priest of our faith, the unspotted sacrifice who has cleansed us of our sins, who by offering himself has purified a corrupted world. . . . Lord God of all, you are pleased with an offering of thanksgiving from those who come before you with a sincere good will; graciously receive this offering of incense given by your undeserving servants. Grant us greater worthiness to approach your holy altar; give us grace to offer a victim and a spiritual sacrifice for our offenses and the faults of all your people; be pleased to approve our gifts, pour out your Holy Spirit upon us and upon our offerings and upon all your faithful people, through Jesus Christ our Lord. Amen.*

(Chant of the Priest, Syrian Liturgy)

# 24.

## TRUE EXCHANGE

O GOD, IN A MARVELOUS WAY YOU CREATED HUMAN NATURE, MADE IT NOBLE, AND RENEWED IT STILL MORE WONDERFULLY. GIVE US THE GRACE, BY THE MYSTERY OF THIS WATER AND WINE, TO SHARE IN THE DIVINITY OF THE ONE WHO HUMBLED HIMSELF TO SHARE OUR HUMANITY—JESUS CHRIST, OUR LORD, YOUR SON, LIVING AND REIGNING WITH YOU IN UNION WITH THE HOLY SPIRIT, ONE GOD FOR EVER AND EVER. AMEN.

WE OFFER YOU THE CHALICE OF SALVATION, LORD, WHILE ASKING YOUR MERCY; LET IT ASCEND TO YOUR DIVINE PRESENCE WITH A PLEASING FRAGRANCE, FOR OUR SPIRITUAL WELFARE AND THAT OF THE WHOLE WORLD. AMEN.

*Moses said, 'This is what the Lord orders you to do, that the glory of the Lord may be revealed to you. Come up to the altar,' Moses then told Aaron, 'and offer your sin offering and your holocaust in atonment for yourself and for your family; then present the offering of the people in atonement for them, as the Lord has commanded.' ... Aaron then raised his hands over the people and blessed them. ... Then the glory of the Lord was revealed to all the people. Fire came forth from the Lord's presence and consumed the holocaust and the remnants of the fat on the altar. Seeing this, all the people cried out and fell prostrate. (Leviticus 9:6–7, 22, 42)*

The banquet and the gifts are mere externals of friendship. What is important is that we give of ourselves. This every true friend understands; and every true Christian understands that he must give of himself to God in the Mass. We are human, nevertheless, and we desire to express our love outwardly. We have already done so by accepting Christ's invitation to come to Mass, and by offering the bread and asking his special blessing on it.

It is also customary at a banquet to drink a toast to one another's friendship, to one another's health, success, and happiness. Without intending the slightest irreverence, we might see a comparable ceremony in the mingling of the water and wine at the Offertory of the Mass. The prayer that accompanies this action would seem to indicate such a mutual pledge of friendship and intimacy. For at the mixing of the drops of water with the wine, we pray that "we may have fellowship in the divinity of Jesus Christ, who was pleased to share our humanity." Here is indeed a salute and a pledge of the closest bond of love. Although he is God and infinitely above us, he has come down, emptied himself and become man like us; may we, in this bond of charity, be able to rise and share something of his Godhead.

In the Old Testament the covenant between God and his people, a pledge of friendship and protection and salvation, was sealed by many sacrifices and symbolic ceremonies. Offerings were made to atone for sins and to restore the people to God's favor, and then the Lord sent fire from heaven to show his glory and his approval of the sacrifice.

In the sacrifice of the new law, the offerings of bread and wine are made, with ceremonies of much symbolic meaning, and at the consecration, when the Lord himself becomes present, we are indeed in the presence of his glory and are assured of his good pleasure in the sacrifice of his only-begotten Son.

The divine approval of the New Convenant Sacrifice is symbolized in several ways at the Offertory. In the mixing of the water with the wine we may see the symbol of the divine and human natures in the one person of Jesus Christ, which unites God with man. We may also see the unity between Christ and his Church, the wine indicating the strength of his divine wisdom and perfection, the water which the priest pours into it symbolizing our desire—we are his Church—to partake of the wisdom and the love and the perfect sacrifice of Jesus, to unite ourselves to him, to join ourselves to his work of redemption. St. Paul assures us that Jesus Christ approves of this effort on our part, that we are "to fill up what is yet wanting in the sufferings of Christ" in our own flesh; St. Peter assures the Christian people that they may "rejoice, in so far as you are partakers of the sufferings of Christ, that you may also rejoice in the revelation of his glory" (I Peter 4:13). Thus we share with him the banquet of his sacrifice in a most intimate way.

It was at your word, and your word only, Lord, that this feast of friendship was possible. It was your invitation that began this marvelous exchange, and it is at your consent that we may return this gesture of goodness. No wonder we say, "O God, in a marvelous way you created human nature, made it noble, and renewed it still more wonderfully." Not only have you invited us to your feast. You have allowed us by our own hands to build the house and the banquet table, to lay out the table and prepare the food—the very bread and wine you shall choose to consecrate. . . . No greater dignity could come to any earthly creatures.

We offer the chalice now, the sign of our close bond of friendship with God the Father through Jesus, our mediator.

*Prayer: No one deserves to approach you, O King of glory; no one ought to come near even to bow down and serve you, when he is already enslaved by fleshly desires and pleasures; indeed, to worship you is a service tremendous and awesome even for the angelic Powers of Heaven. And yet your unspeakable and unlimited love for men prompted you to become man; without altering or weakening your divine nature, you became our high priest and as Master of all things created, you brought us the sacred power of offering up this community sacrifice.*

(*Prayer after the Litany of the Faithful, Byzantine Liturgy*)

# 25.

# IN A SPIRIT OF HUMILITY

WITH HUMBLE SPIRIT AND CONVERTED HEART MAY WE BE ACCEPTABLE
TO YOU, LORD; MAY OUR SACRIFICE TODAY BE OFFERED BEFORE YOU IN A
MANNER THAT PLEASES YOU, LORD GOD.

COME, O SANCTIFIER, ALL-POWERFUL, ETERNAL GOD, AND BLESS THIS
SACRIFICE PREPARED TO HONOR YOUR HOLY NAME.

*In a contrite heart and humble spirit let us be accepted. As in
holocausts of rams and bullocks, and as in thousands of fat lambs,
so let our sacrifice be made in thy sight this day, that it may please
thee, for there is no confusion to them that trust in thee. (Daniel
3:39–40)*

When invited to the home of a great dignitary, we consider it
simple good manners to remember who we are and take care to
"keep our place," as the saying goes. This gracious respect for our
host is a virtue attractive to everyone. If a king or president would
invite us to his table, it would be no more than right for us to
recognize his generosity in doing so, and we would not abuse the
occasion by boldly trying "to run the show." We know he has
honored us; we cannot dishonor him by any conduct that wouldn't
show our deepest appreciation.

At the Offertory of the Mass, we mingled water and wine, symbolizing our joy at being allowed to partake in the divinity of Jesus, who generously gave himself to our humanity. But let us not for a moment forget who has given the greater gift, who has done the greater favor, who deserves the greater honor. We were made his intimates, but that is no reason for becoming rash.

In the prayers that follow the offering of the chalice, as well as the prayer of offering itself, the Church seems to nudge us out of our ecstasy. It is not really we (the water) that have mingled with Christ (the wine). It is you, Jesus, who have descended to us. It would not do for us to forget our place and take unfair advantage of your generosity. Therefore, when we offered the chalice we did it "while asking your mercy," and we hoped that through your greatness the cup of wine we offered would be pleasing "in your divine majesty," in your most holy and "divine presence." We must not forget, it is the greatest and most majestic of all presences.

"With humble spirit and converted heart may we be acceptable to you, Lord." It is not our own excellence which will make this banquet a success. It is not our worthiness which will make our gift adequate. There can be no real exchange—neither our offering nor the abundant favors you return us—based on our own merits. Only you, Lord, by your gracious love, can make the gifts suitable, both what we give and what we receive. Only you can assure us that what we have done is worthy of your friendship. These conclusions are essential to our self-knowledge as your creatures. Therefore we pray, "Come, O Sanctifier, almighty, everlasting God, and bless these sacrificial gifts, prepared for the glory of your holy name." You alone make all things eternally good, beautiful, noble, and life-giving.

*Prayer: O God, Lord of us all, you have sent the Bread of Heaven down to us, food to give life to the whole earth, our God and Master, Jesus Christ, to bring blessings and make us holy. Bless this sacrifice yourself, Lord, and accept it on your holy altar in heaven. Guard us in your keeping, to complete this service of your divine mysteries, so we may serve you with pure hearts and do homage to your glorious name, Father, Son, and Holy Spirit, today and forever and through all eternity. Amen.*

(*Offertory Prayer, Ruthenian Liturgy*)

# 26.

## I WILL WASH

*I wash my hands in innocence, and I go around your altar, O Lord, giving voice to my thanks, and recounting all your wondrous deeds. O Lord, I love the house in which you dwell, the tenting-place of your glory. Gather not my soul with those of sinners, nor with men of blood my life. On their hands are crimes, and their right hands are full of bribes. But I walk in integrity; redeem me and have pity on me. My foot stands on level ground; in the assemblies I will bless the Lord. (Psalm 25:6 ff.)*

This prayer for the purification rite of the Mass is a direct quotation from Psalm 25. The "Lavabo" of the Mass, in which the priest symbolically washes his hands for all of us, has many meanings, just as water itself has many uses.

We have been invited to the divine table for a meeting of God's friends, and the celebration of a love-feast. At this great event Jesus will be present and will give himself, Body and Blood, to God the Father for us. This total surrender of the One most perfect, most spotless and beautiful among men, will win for us endless blessings and will bring us good things beyond number.

The least we can do is offer ourselves with our loyalty and love in return. But as we look at ourselves—like guests taking a quick glance in the mirror before the banquet—we are fully aware that we are ill-prepared for making such a presentation. So we hasten to a wash-basin to cleanse ourselves; this need for inner purification and preparation is our reason for describing Purgatory as we do, as the place of cleansing afforded the souls of our departed brethren to ready them for the eternal banquet of heaven.

Purifying ceremonies like the "Lavabo" of the Mass come most naturally and fittingly to intelligent Christians. A man who knows what life is all about, who knows God and himself—and knows the difference—is constantly in the process of purifying himself. The Church is aware of this need, and employs water generously as a symbol of it. From the initiating rite of baptism, when our foreheads are washed in the sign of the Holy Trinity, to the sprinkling of the casket at our grave, the Church keeps reminding us how pure a soul must be, to come into the presence of God.

At Sunday High Mass we have the *Asperges,* in which we are sprinkled with holy water, purified as we enter the sacred house of God and begin the holy sacrifice. As children we were taught the frequent use of holy water "to chase the devil away," which is really just another way of emphasizing our need for spiritual cleansing.

Well may we thank God for a similar ceremony at the Mass, the most important invitation to the most sacred of banquets, in a friendship most intimate, with the Friend most high and holy! What innocence should we not bring to this privileged table! As we say the words with the priest, "I wash my hands among the innocent," how easy it is to recall that we have just asked for "the spirit of humility and a contrite heart." We are far from innocent, but may the spirit of genuine contrition, at least, help bring us nearer to a restored innocence. Surely we must be purged into a thorough, complete innocence before we can become sharers in the eternal banquet.

*Prayer: Lord, purify my unclean soul; wash me in the waters of life to make me worthy to enter your Holy of Holies pure and just; then may I offer you a life-giving sacrifice which pleases your divine majesty and which resembles your glorious self-offering for us, Lord God. . . . O God, blot out our sins, pardon and wash us clean of our offenses and negligences, forgive the sins of all who return to you and petition you with a genuine spirit of faith. Remember, O God, our ancestors, our brothers in Christ, our superiors, and all souls who have passed into eternity placing their hope in you; remember, finally, all the living and dead for whom we offer this sacrifice.*

(*Lavabo Prayer, Syrian Liturgy*)

# 27.

## RECEIVE, O HOLY TRINITY

RECEIVE THIS OFFERING, O HOLY TRINITY, WHICH WE PRESENT TO YOU IN MEMORY OF THE SUFFERINGS, RESURRECTION AND ASCENSION OF JESUS CHRIST OUR LORD; AND IN HONOR OF BLESSED MARY EVER VIRGIN, OF BLESSED JOHN THE BAPTIST, OF THE HOLY APOSTLES PETER AND PAUL —IN HONOR OF THESE AND ALL THE SAINTS. LET IT BE FOR THEIR GLORY AND OUR ETERNAL SALVATION; MAY THEY INTERCEDE FOR US IN HEAVEN AS WE CHERISH THEIR MEMORY ON EARTH, THROUGH THE SAME CHRIST OUR LORD. AMEN.

*After this I saw a great multitude which no man could number, out of all nations and tribes and peoples and tongues, standing before the throne and before the Lamb, clothed in white robes, and with palms in their hands. And they cried with a loud voice, saying, Salvation belongs to our God who sits upon the throne, and to the Lamb. (Apocalypse 7–9:10)*

No gift, however poor or small, is ever rejected by a loving parent. There are two reasons why a mother and father treasure even a wilted bouquet given them by their small children. First because of the children's love (that has prompted them to make the offering), and second because of the parents' love (that makes them constantly grateful for the children).

*88*

For these reasons, too, we anticipate God's pleasure in our poor offerings. Not because the bread and wine or any other goods we have offered God are of such value themselves as to be worthy of him. It is our love, our self-surrender to God's goodness that is important, "for the gift without the giver is bare." But even the offering of our very selves is not enough. It is the love of our Father in heaven that gives true value and meaning to our gifts; and it is that love which takes the gift of bread and wine and turns it into the infinitely perfect gift. From our side, our deepest appreciation must accompany the offering—all our joys and sorrows, our fears and hopes, our generous good works and our struggles with temptation. All of this and our very life should go with "this offering . . . which we present" to the Holy Trinity with this prayer.

Our gift must bear with it our poor love at its best; this gives it meaning as the child's love turns the wilted bouquet into a heavenly charm to please its parents. Yet it is really God's infinite love that gives the offering its real significance. How wisely the Church in the closing prayers of the Offertory reminds the Holy Trinity of what God's love has done for us, rather than what we or our love have done for him: "Receive our offering, Holy Trinity," we pray, not for any greatness of ours, not for any worthiness we claim, but because of your overwhelming love for us, "in memory of the sufferings, resurrection and ascension of our Lord Jesus Christ."

And if we must boast of the love and gratitude our human race has shown its Creator, at least we will not boast of our own. We have far too little good in us for any pride; yet we can rejoice in some of our race who truly pleased you, who truly offered you the best that man has accomplished, such as the "blessed Mary, ever virgin, John the Baptist, the holy apostles Peter and Paul, and indeed, all the saints." These were your friends and they are ours; they are the best of our kind. They give us confidence in your goodness and the power of your grace. Let these our gifts, then, bring "honor to the saints and salvation to us." May "they plead for us in heaven" when we so often fail on earth.

*Prayer: Let us send up our praise to the most glorious Trinity at
every instant forever. Christ was sacrificed for our redemption and
requested that we make the remembrance of his death and burial
and resurrection; may he then receive this sacrifice we make, taking
it from our hands by his grace and loving kindness. Amen. Lord,
God of us all, by your instruction these sublime and blessed and
life-giving and heavenly mysteries are laid out on the altar of reparation, until the second coming of our Lord from heaven; to him be
glory for all ages. Amen. Let us remember the Virgin Mary, Mother
of God, at this blessed altar. Let us pray now and always that the
blessing of peace may pervade the universe; thus pray, O apostles
of the Son of God, you who loved the Only-begotten One. . . . Let
us remember on the holy altar all just souls who have won the
victory and all the martyrs who have received their crown.*

                              *(The Diptychs, Chaldean Liturgy)*

# 28.

## PRAY, BRETHREN

Pray, brethren, that my sacrifice and yours may be acceptable
to God the Father almighty. May the Lord receive the sacrifice
from your hands, to the praise and glory of his name, to our
benefit also, and the good of all his holy Church. Amen.

*May the Lord send you help from the sanctuary, from Sion may
he sustain you. May he remember all your offerings and graciously
accept your holocaust. May he grant you what is in your heart and
fulfill your every plan. (Psalm 19:3–5)*

*This atonement is to be made by the priest who has been anointed
and ordained to the priesthood in succession to his father. He shall
wear the linen garments, the sacred vestments, and make atonement
for the sacred sanctuary, the Meeting Tent and the altar, as well as
for the priests and all the people of the community. (Leviticus
17:32–33)*

It seems strange, at first, that when we have just been following
the Offertory of the Mass so closely with the priest, when we have
offered ourselves with the bread and wine to God our Father, when
we have brought our joys and sorrows to him, and laid our talents,
our successes and failures at his feet—it seems surprising, if not an
insult, to see the priest turn to us and hear him tell us, "Pray,
brethren."

But as we follow the prayer of the priest, we see it is a fitting conclusion to the offering we have made of ourselves, the desire we have expressed to give our lives to God as true Christians. It comes as a refrain or chorus. The Offertory prayers have been said in silence, and now we speak out loud to each other, priest and people, to make sure we are in agreement. We are like a closely-knit group in a room, thinkly silently on a subject for a time, then telling each other of our conclusions. Or we might say, just in case we have been distracted at this important part of the Mass, that the priest reminds us that this is our last chance to get ourselves into the sacrifice, to put the giver into the gift. And we then answer, "We are with you; we are aware of what we are to do in these sacred moments."

The prayer which we say so "that our sacrifice may become acceptable" is the prayer over the gifts, the prayer that concludes the offering of the gifts to God, gathered especially in the real and symbolic offering of the bread and wine, which by divine institution are to become the perfect sacrifice, the Body and Blood of the Redeemer. The concluding "prayer over the gifts" or "the Secret prayer," since it is said silently, is changeable according to the various Sundays and feasts, as are also the "prayer of the assembly" and the prayer which concludes the Communion part of the Mass. Coming as it does at the end of the Offertory, it is expressive of our intentions and petitions, our purpose in offering the gifts and our hope for their sanctification and ratification. So we pray, "Lord, accept the gifts we bring you; may they make us worthy to receive your grace in return." So in a festive spirit we ask, "May our offering, may this sacrifice make us worthy to celebrate this feastday and its holy season as your true and loyal sons; may we have a part in the perfect sacrifice of your glorious only-begotten Son."

*Prayer: May our offering on today's feast be pleasing to you, Lord. In your gracious kindness may this exchange of sacred gifts make us grow to be more like him in whom our human nature has been joined to you.*

*Lord, may our gifts today be appropriate to the mystery of your birth, and bring us peace for all time. As this child who was born man was also resplendent with the divine nature, so may our offering of earthly material serve to bring us closer to what is divine, through the same Lord Jesus Christ....*

*Sanctify the gifts we offer you, Lord, on the new birth of your only-begotten Son, and cleanse us completely from the stains of our sins. Through our Lord Jesus Christ your Son.*

*(Secret Prayers for the Three Masses of Christmas,*
*Roman Missal)*

# 29.

## HYMN OF THANKS

TRULY IT IS PROPER AND JUST, FITTING AND TO OUR BENEFIT TO THANK YOU ALWAYS AND EVERYWHERE, HOLY LORD, ALL-POWERFUL FATHER, ETERNAL GOD, THROUGH CHRIST OUR LORD. THROUGH HIM THE ANGELS PRAISE YOUR MAJESTY, THE DOMINATIONS ADORE YOU, THE HEAVENLY POWERS TREMBLE BEFORE YOU. THE ARMY OF HEAVEN'S VIRTUES JOINS WITH THE HOLY SERAPHIM IN A FESTIVE SONG OF PRAISE. WE PRAY THAT OUR VOICES MAY BLEND WITH THEIRS AS ALL UNITED WE SING OUR PROCLAMATION.

*Be filled with the Spirit, speaking to one another in psalms and hymns and spiritual songs, singing and making melody in your hearts to the Lord, giving thanks always for all things in the name of our Lord Jesus Christ to God the Father. (Ephesians 5:19-20)*

*I will give you thanks in the vast assembly, in the mighty throng I will praise you. (Psalm 34:18)*

*Give thanks to the Lord, for he is good, for his mercy endures forever. (Psalm 135:1)*

The Book of Psalms, divinely inspired prayerbook of the Old Testament, contains a great number of joyous thanksgiving hymns. Words of gratitude to God are the sign of a healthy soul. If we find ourselves filled with a spiritual joy that spills over into habitual thoughts and words of thanks to God, it is very likely that we have come to know and love God in a real sense, and that we are in good spiritual condition.

If not, it is the Church's aim to put us into that state of soul. In the Preface to the Canon of the Mass, we are instructed on the manner of approaching God, now that he is so near.

At the Mass we are like children who do not quite understand what is being given us. Our true appreciation has hardly awakened. "What do you say, Johnny?" asks an anxious mother. Her little Johnny is awkwardly speechless before his godfather, a generous uncle who has just given him a huge package, a birthday gift. An embarrassing pause. . . . Suddenly Johnny blushes and mumbles, "thank you," and everyone sighs with relief. Johnny has said the right word; he is not ungrateful after all; he appreciates the gift— or at least he once had a lesson in good manners.

We who are always teaching gratitude to our children often think so little of it ourselves! At the Mass—admittedly a mystery quite above us—we are like small children receiving the huge unknown, the great, mysterious gift package. We know by rote that the Mass is a source of endless graces, but these are mere words to us until we have intensified our spiritual life enough to experience the real working of grace.

So it is to a double gratitude that the Church calls us in the Preface of the Mass. We must first be grateful to God before we discover his gifts. We must appreciate the beauty of life itself, the joy of innocence and goodness, the glory and dignity of being God's creatures—and indeed his very children. We must first "lift up our hearts" before we understand how much has been given. Like the young child, we must open the parcel and examine the gift. Then a new and real gratitude will arise within us. Each expression of thanks—and there are many in the Mass—should have more meaning than the last. Gratitude itself will be more important to us each time we utter an expression of it.

*Prayer: It is fitting and right to sing of you, to speak well of you with words of praise and gratitude, to adore you everywhere throughout your dominion. For you are the inexpressible, incomprehensible, invisible God, great beyond our knowledge, eternally undiminished, with your only-begotten Son and your Holy Spirit. You have led us forth from nothingness into being; you have raised us up out of a fallen condition; you have left nothing undone to lead us on to Heaven to your kingdom which is yet to come. We return thanks to you and to your only Son and to your Holy Spirit for all these blessings and for all your goodness to us, whether known or unknown to us, whether clear to us or concealed. We thank you also for your gracious acceptance of this offering from our hands. And now around your throne are legions of archangels and countless angels, cherubim and seraphim, with the six wings and the many eyes; they are carried on high by their wings as they sing, raising their voices and proclaiming a great song of triumph.*

*(The Preface, Byzantine Mass)*

# 29,b.

## HOLY, HOLY, HOLY

Holy, Holy, Holy Lord God of the heavenly armies! Heaven and earth are filled with your glory! Hosanna in the highest! Blessed is he who is coming as the witness of the Lord! Hosanna in the highest!

*I saw the Lord sitting upon a throne high and elevated: and his train filled the temple. Upon it stood the seraphims: the one had six wings, and the other had six wings: with two they covered his face, and with two they covered his feet, and with two they flew. And they cried one to another and said: Holy, Holy, Holy, the Lord God of hosts, all the earth is full of his glory. And the lintels of the doors were moved at the voice of him that cried, and the house was filled with smoke. And I said: Woe is me, because I have held my peace; because I am a man of unclean lips . . . and I have seen with my eyes the King the Lord of hosts. (Isaias 6:1–5)*

*And when he was drawing near, being by now at the descent of the Mount of Olives, the whole company of the disciples began to rejoice and to praise God with a loud voice for all the miracles that they had seen, saying, 'Blessed is he who comes as king, in the name of the Lord! Peace in heaven, and glory in the highest!' (Luke 19:37–38)*

The great Thanksgiving Song ends in a burst of glory and brilliance: "Holy, holy, holy Lord God of the heavenly armies! Heaven and earth are filled with your glory!" We are in the temple of God, about to call him down into our midst in his real, sacramental presence. The bread and wine of the sacrifice have been offered. Our souls have been purified and prepared for the most sacred moment, when the offerings shall lose themselves, and earth shall give way to heaven.

For the introduction to this solemn moment, the Church has chosen that beautiful and terrible and awe-inspiring scene in the glorious temple of Jerusalem, the vision of Isaias. As the temple was made holy by this sublime vision, so will our church be made holy at the consecration, when the same Lord, the same God, the Son in the person of Jesus Christ, shall again fill this place and make it sacred with his divine presence.

The Church has beautifully combined the words of God in Isaias with the New Testament words of the people when God himself entered the holy city on Palm Sunday, when the Redeemer came to his own, meek and humble and clothed with simplicity and poverty, but nonetheless royal and divine. "Blessed is he who comes as king, in the name of the Lord!"

So now shall he enter our city and this hallowed place, meek and lowly, but no less divine and powerful. What a glorious combination of scenes, what a magnificent paradox: God both great and humble shall be with us; God both powerful and small; immensely rich, yet pitifully poor; tremendous and exalted, yet most lovable and approachable. Both scenes, and the words and thoughts they convey, belong in the Mass, for they belong in our hearts at the threshold of the consecration.

*Prayer: Holy, holy, holy is the Lord, the all-powerful God. Heaven and earth are filled with his glory, with his being, with his sublime majesty: "for heaven and earth are full of my presence," says the Lord. Holiness is yours, O God, true Father; all fatherhood on earth derives from yours in heaven. Holiness is yours, Holy Spirit;*

*all created things are sanctified at your bidding. Alas! Woe is me!*
*I tremble, for my eyes have seen the omnipotent King and Master,*
*though I am a man of unsanctified lips, with the world surrounding*
*my life. How awesome is this spot, where this very day I behold the*
*Lord face to face! It is no less than the house of God and the entry-*
*gate of heaven. Grant, Lord, that we may be filled with your grace.*

(*Prayer before the Consecration, Chaldean Liturgy*)

# 30.

## THAT ALL MAY BE ONE

FATHER MOST MERCIFUL, WE HUMBLY PETITION YOU THROUGH JESUS
CHRIST YOUR SON, OUR MASTER; WE ASK YOU TO ACCEPT AND TO BLESS
THESE GIFTS, THESE TOKENS, THESE HOLY, UNBLEMISHED OFFERINGS. WE
ARE OFFERING THEM TO YOU IN THE FIRST PLACE FOR YOUR HOLY
CATHOLIC CHURCH; GUARD, GUIDE, AND GOVERN HER IN PEACE THROUGH-
OUT THE WORLD. WE OFFER THEM WITH YOUR SERVANT OUR POPE N.,
AND OUR BISHOP N., AND ALL FAITHFUL TEACHERS OF THE CATHOLIC
AND APOSTOLIC FAITH.

*Not for these only do I pray, but for those also who through their
word are to believe in me, that all may be one, even as thou, Father,
in me and I in thee; that they also may be one in us, that the world
may believe that thou has sent me. (John 17:20–21)*

As we approach this most divine moment of the day, this joining
place between heaven and earth, let no one be forgotten. All things
belong to him, all must be covered with his blessing and have its
original holiness renewed. But we, the creatures he endowed with
free will, are in greatest need of blessing. For we have abused that
freedom, wrongly taken it to hide ourselves from him and seek
what is far inferior to him—inferior even to our own natures. We
have greatest need to be brought back into his presence.

Moreover, the Holy Eucharist is the divine banquet for the family

of men. It is not a private devotion so much as the solemn meeting
of faithful Christians, just as the Last Supper itself had been the
official meeting of Jesus with his Apostles, and as the early "Breaking of the Bread" brought together the growing Church he had
founded. So as the bread of man is about to become the Bread of
Heaven, the children of God must be gathered from the ends of the
earth. The Church, aware of this duty, places six remembrances
around the central act of the Mass: three before it and three after it.

"Since we partake of one bread, we all become the one body and
blood of Christ and members of one another," wrote St. John
Damascene of this closely-knit union. While we begin here the part
of the Mass that is most intimate, and in a real sense most personal,
we are at the same time at an event most public and world-wide.
None of us can feel like an isolated hermit in a mountain cave, com-
municating with God alone. Rather, we have all the world crowded
around us. Like the Jews of old, we have come to Jerusalem from
the four corners of the earth to the solemn sacrifice of the temple.
This paradox follows from the one we have just meditated on (at
the Sanctus). It derives from the infinite nature of God himself,
who is all to all and everything to each, who is most personal and
most universal, most intimate to every creature and most public to
all creation; so also is the Church he founded, and the Bread of
Heaven, with which he feeds it.

First of the six commemorations is the large, general one, after
which we shall become more specific, praying with the Church for
the living on earth, the souls in Purgatory, ourselves (we sinners),
and all creatures of God. In the midst of these prayers we shall
several times pay honor to the saints.

"Father most merciful, through Jesus Christ your Son, we ask you
to accept and to bless the gifts which we have placed on the altar."
Our gifts at the Offertory were to present and represent our good
will, our love, our whole selves. The Mass is an offering of love.
Our whole effort thus far has been to make our offering more and
more worthy: our best is not enough, but it is required.

The infinite gift which is soon to surround us is world-wide; if

any spiritual work is to make us world-conscious, it is surely the
Mass. The sacrifice into which we are now to enter—both giving and
receiving at the same time—is not only intended for all Christians
and indeed all men; it is the best the world has to offer—past,
present, or future. It is the eternal Son of God descending to us, to
be our gift to God (since he is one of us, a man) and God's gift to
us (since he is the Divine Person, equal to the Father and the Holy
Spirit). No wonder that at the beginning of the solemn Canon of
the Mass, we pray, "we offer this holy and spotless gift for the entire
Church throughout the world."

*Prayer: We implore of your kindness, of the love you bear man-
kind, to remember your one, holy, catholic and apostolic Church . . .
spread through the earth from end to end. Pour your blessing upon
all nations and make fertile the fields. Shed your grace on rulers
and their armies, on counsellors and ambassadors, on our people
and our neighboring lands, on our entries and exits. Bring harmony
to them, O King of Peace, and give us the blessing of your friendship. All that we possess you have given us; O God, receive us as
your possession, for we know no other God. On your holy name
we call. Let our lives be directed by your Holy Spirit; let no poison
of sin ever enslave the servants who belong to you. Again let us
implore your kindness, lover of men, to remember our holy father
and chief sacred ruler, Pope N., our most reverend father and
patriarch, N., and their fellow-servant, our bishop, N.*

*(Memento, Coptic Liturgy)*

# 31.

## REMEMBER THE LIVING

REMEMBER, LORD, YOUR SERVANTS, MEN AND WOMEN. . . [THE PRIEST NAMES THOSE FOR WHOM HE SPECIALLY PRAYS TODAY] AND ALL WHO ARE GATHERED AROUND YOUR ALTAR. THEIR FAITH AND DEVOTION IS KNOWN TO YOU.

*To this end also we pray always for you, that our God may make you worthy of his calling, and may fulfill with power every good purpose and work of faith, that the name of our Lord Jesus Christ may be glorified in you, and you in him, according to the grace of our God and the Lord Jesus Christ. (II Thess. 1:11-12)*

> No man is an island,
> No man stands alone.

Thus the words of a popular song. Proud and independent as a man may be, his destiny is never purely of his own making. His way to heaven or to hell is not paved by himself alone, any more than he expects a highway to be the product of a solitary worker. Whichever direction we go, we are brought there in part by our fellowmen, and we in turn drag others about with us.

Marriage counsellors say that husband and wife make their way *together* toward happiness or misery; sociologists say that environment—the whole scheme of home, friendships, associations, hero-worship, community customs—means so much to the character formation of a child (and an adult as well); studies and experiences of psychiatrists point to mental illness as being a family symptom as much as an individual one. It should come as a smaller surprise to find that we can never be spiritually isolated.

Witness the great power wielded unwittingly by a great, saintly, generous man or woman with an outgoing personality. Such a person's qualities not only merit a good reputation and the admiration of his acquaintances; they change the very lives of his friends, so that their whole attitude and outlook are powerfully influenced. It has often been said that nothing has so profound an effect upon one's thoughts and actions, one's mode of life, as to live with a saint. But this is merely an outward manifestation of what goes on spiritually in the human family.

It is in the Body of Christ, the great mysterious and very real unity, that our good works powerfully affect others. This is a most important Catholic doctrine, strongly and clearly preached by Jesus and the apostles. Many images and comparisons were used by them to clarify the notion of this mystic union—in so far as a mystery can be clarified, for every good illumination of a mystery deepens it, opens the way to more mysteries. Our union with all the faithful is likened to that of a *family*: we are called "the sons of God." We are called "citizens with the saints and members of God's household." We are spoken of as stones in a *building* with "Christ Jesus as the corner stone." Jesus likens our union with him to that of the "vine and the branches," in which all our good work affects others through him, the *vine*. But especially, we are called "a living *body*." We are "the body of Christ, member for member, with Christ at the head." How, then, could we forget the other members of Christ at this solemn festival?

*Prayer: United let us ask the Lord God with full heart to bless us with brotherhood in the Holy Spirit. . . . May we become mem-*

*bers of one another by the Holy Spirit and perfected by this sacrifice
and worthy to live in God forever and ever. Amen. . . . Send the
grace of your Holy Spirit into our souls.*

*(Prayer at the Breaking of the Host, Ethiopic Liturgy)*

# 3 1,b.

## FOR ALL WHO OFFER

FOR THEM WE OFFER OR THEY THEMSELVES OFFER THIS SACRIFICE OF
PRAISE FOR THEIR OWN GOOD AND THE GOOD OF ALL THEY HOLD DEAR,
FOR THE REDEMPTION OF THEIR SOULS, FOR THE HOPE OF SALVATION AND
WELL-BEING. THEY DEDICATE THEMSELVES TO YOU, THE ETERNAL, LIVING
AND TRUE GOD.

*Offer to God praise as your sacrifice and fulfill your vows to the
Most High; then call upon me in time of distress; I will rescue you,
and you shall glorify me. (Psalm 49:14-15)*

*For just as in one body we have many members, yet all the mem-
bers have not the same function, so we, the many, are one body in
Christ, but severally members of one another. (Romans 12:4-5)*

Much goes on in the world around us without our knowledge.
The movements of the solar systems, the flight of meteors through
space, the action of atomic energy, the birth and life and death of
uncounted creatures on this earth—yes, even our own physical and
mental growth and our life itself—all are mysteries for the most part
hidden from us. Yet the well-ordered work of nature continues
fruitfully, whether we are aware of it or not. There is endless beauty
and goodness and love and power in the universe around us,
whether we notice it or not.

But obviously it is to our advantage in every way to know more and more about these marvels of creation. Our own pleasure and happiness and fullness of nature depends upon our increasing awareness and understanding of the universe and all it contains. So it is in the Mystical Body of Christ. Our good works, our virtues and degree of grace do benefit the other members of Christ, whether we realize it or not. For that is the nature of Christ's Body, the Church. But how deep and rich our spiritual life becomes as we probe further into this marvelous mystery with St. Paul: "There are indeed many members, yet but one body. And the eye cannot say to the hand, 'I do not need thy help,' nor the head to the feet, 'I have no need of you.' . . . If one member suffers anything, all the members suffer with it, or if one member glories, all the members rejoice with it. Now you are the body of Christ, member for member" (I Corinthians 12:21–27).

To know of our intimate spiritual connection with our neighbor is of immense value to our life of prayer; it is, rather, essential to our correct participation in the Mass. Our presence at Mass is not just another "visit to the Blessed Sacrament," another hour of meditation, or another round of "favorite devotions" or emotions, however good and praiseworthy they may be in themselves. The Mass is a sacrifice on our part in the sense of a total gift, a surrender of self and personal desires in order to be offered to God in community with our brethren. That is why the prayers of the Mass so often make mention of the salvation of the whole world.

Here, in the special remembrance of the living, we ask God for blessings in particular on the devout Christians who have learned to share the Mass with Christ, "whose faith and devotion are known" to him, who "themselves offer to you this sacrifice of praise," and "who dedicate themselves to you, the eternal, living and true God." They, the most healthy members of Christ on this earth, have a special right to our attention.

*Prayer: Lord, remember this city in which we live; be mindful of every city and country in which your faithful make their homes. Lord, remember sailors at sea and other travellers, the sick and suf-*

*fering, and prisoners; be mindful of their salvation. Lord, remember
the faithful who bring offerings to you in the churches you make
holy; remember those who have been kind to us and those who are
helpful to the poor; pour down your mercies on all of us.*

(*Commemorations, Byzantine Mass*)

# 32.

## THE SAINTS AT MASS

WE HONOR AND REMEMBER AND UNITE IN CLOSE FRIENDSHIP WITH FIRST
THE GLORIOUS MARY, VIRGIN FOREVER, MOTHER OF OUR GOD AND LORD
JESUS CHRIST; BLESSED JOSEPH, SPOUSE OF THIS VIRGIN; THEN YOUR
BLESSED APOSTLES AND MARTYRS: PETER AND PAUL, ANDREW, JAMES,
JOHN, THOMAS, JAMES, PHILIP, BARTHOLOMEW, MATTHEW, SIMON AND
THADDEUS; LINUS, CLETUS, CLEMENT, SIXTUS, CORNELIUS, CYPRIAN,
LAWRENCE, CHRYSOGONUS, JOHN AND PAUL, COSMAS AND DAMIAN,
AND WE RECALL ALL OF YOUR SAINTS. THROUGH THEIR GOOD DEEDS AND
PRAYERS GRANT US YOUR HELP AND DEFENSE AND PROTECTION. THROUGH
THE SAME CHRIST OUR LORD. AMEN.

*You are now no longer strangers and foreigners, but you are
citizens with the saints and members of God's household: you are
built upon the foundation of the apostles and prophets with Christ
Jesus himself as the chief corner stone. In him the whole structure
is closely fitted together and grows into a temple holy in the Lord;
in him you too are being built together into a dwelling place for
God in the Spirit. (Ephesians 2:19-22)*

After remembering the whole Church, her leaders and faithful
throughout the world, and those in the faith who are dear to us, we
turn to the saints in heaven, mentioning many of them by name.

Why bring all the saints into the Mass? Because the Church herself, who offers this sacrifice for us and in us, is the Communion of Saints. In this the Church differs from every other organization on earth. She stretches far beyond matter and time. We are accustomed to saying that all earthly ties are broken at the hour of death, that "you can't take it with you," and that if you are a "deceased member" of a club or society, you are only a memory, a thing of the past. But all this is not true in the Church of Christ, for the Church extends firmly into eternity; her ties with the next world are complete and active, and, in fact, she is more concerned with what comes after death than what comes before; the Church considers this life principally as a preparation for the next.

Thus a good Christian at prayer constantly penetrates through the veil of this material world into the heaven toward which he aspires *now*, not merely at the end of life. A good Christian at Mass is aware of his fellow-parishioners on earth and of his fellowmen in heaven as well. The greatest of these fellowmen—brothers and sisters in Christ—are the great saints, the holiest of the holy ones. How naturally his mind comes to them at Mass! They are the living images of Christ.

The relics of the saints are kept in the altar stone as a special reminder of our union with heaven. Heaven sanctifies the altar, Christ and his entire heavenly court. Symbols and relics are aids to human memory and human attention. We are always saying, "This reminded me of you." Not all Christian symbols or images may suit our aesthetic tastes, but the underlying truth they represent is so important, so beautiful and inspiring, that we can in no way afford to miss it. The Communion of Saints in Christ, the great family of God, is the paradise and the fulfillment of joy for which we were created. This should not be too hard for us to believe, if we have ever experienced the joy of happy family life and happy associations with our friends on earth.

The saints are members of Jesus in the fullest sense; they are most filled with his life; they are the healthiest members of the Mystical Body. Their strength flows on into the other members—us on earth as well. It is not idle dreaming to imagine the saints surrounding the altar at Mass, present with us, loving and worshipping with us. They are, after all, most intimate members of Christ. They are most deeply interested in his every action.

*Prayer: Lord, remember us and have compassion on us. We pray that Blessed Mary ever Virgin, Mother of God, John the Baptist, Stephen the First Martyr, Gregory the Lightbearer and all the saints may be remembered in the sacrifice of this sacred offering. Be mindful of them, O Lord, and merciful to us. We pray that all the holy apostles, prophets, teachers and martyrs, all holy rulers of the Church, bishops of the apostolic succession, faithful priests and deacons, and all the saints may be reverently remembered in this holy sacrifice.*

(*Commemoration of the Armenian Liturgy*)

# 33.

## HIS OWN HOUSEHOLD

THIS OFFERING OF OUR SERVICE AND OF YOUR WHOLE FAMILY, LORD,
WE ASK YOU TO ACCEPT WITH PLEASURE. REGULATE OUR DAYS IN YOUR
PEACE, RESCUE US FROM ETERNAL DOOM, AND ARRANGE TO COUNT US
AMONG THE COMPANY OF YOUR CHOSEN. THROUGH CHRIST OUR LORD.
AMEN.

*And he said to me, 'These are they who have come out of the great
tribulation, and have washed their robes and have made them white
in the blood of the Lamb. Therefore they are before the throne of
God, and serve him day and night in his temple, and he who sits
upon the throne will dwell with them.'* (Apocalypse 7:14-15)

"We ask you to accept this offering of our service and of your
whole family," says the priest as he spreads his hands over the bread
and wine, and the bell is rung to warn us of the approaching
moment of consecration. "Our service and that of your whole
family. . . ." With what tender intimacy the Church leads us to
Calvary, to Christ's offering there, and through him to our Father
in heaven!

Is it true that we can "be of service" to God? Does he need us
at all? The thought seems impossible, yet mysteriously encouraging.
For when you love someone, you wish, not that he will suffer need

and be forced to call on you for help, but that somehow you can do something very great for him.

Is it not for this very great human desire in us that Jesus revealed the awful mystery of his thirst, of his longing for our love? Here is the puzzle to confound all puzzles. How is it that he could empty himself so much as to need us? "You are the ones who have been faithful to me in my trials," he said to his apostles, and promised them a place beside him at table in his kingdom, as having been *friends in need*.

Who can understand the frightening self-effacement of the Son of God? He pleads for our help, after willfully and deliberately making us free to accept or reject that plea! What greater honor could he have given us? We are the chosen children of his family, we are his household! So this prayer of the Mass reminds us. Strange indictment of human callousness—that we must be reminded, once we have heard the stunning truth!

We are, in truth, his family; we have just one prayer ago boldly joined ourselves with the company of the saints in heaven. Boldly, but it has given us confidence; it has almost made us secure. The saints are those Christians who have most perfectly "fulfilled in their bodies what was lacking in the sufferings of Christ," as we hear in that mystifying statement of St. Paul.

Yes, Jesus in his love and his desire to let us share with him a part of the household, held back something of his infinite saving power. Like a loving elder brother, he "let us do something, too," gave us a real share in his all-important work. Infinite love can devise infinite, mysterious means to share love. It is the most noble action of our free will to assume an active role in Christ's redemption, in imitation of his mother Mary when she said, "Be it done to me as you have said." Christ has truly redeemed all, but by our free, loving "yes" and our cooperation, we apply that redemption to ourselves and to others.

*Prayer: May he descend and bless and sanctify this offering; Lord, may it win for us remission of our sins and pardon for our offences;*

*may it nourish our hope of resurrection from death and glorified life
in the realm of heaven, in company with your servants who led holy
and godly lives in your sight. We give thanks to you for your marvelous providence in dealing with us; we praise you forever in your holy
Church, cleansed and saved in the precious blood of Christ.*

(*Prayers before the Consecration, Liturgy of Malabar*)

# 34.

## CAN IT REALLY BE?

BE PLEASED, O GOD, TO MAKE THIS OFFERING IN ALL WAYS BLESSED, CONSECRATED, APPROVED, REASONABLE AND ACCEPTABLE, SO THAT IT MAY BECOME FOR US THE BODY AND BLOOD OF YOUR DEARLY LOVED SON, OUR LORD JESUS CHRIST.

*For my flesh is food indeed, and my blood is drink indeed. He who eats my flesh and drinks my blood abides in me and I in him. As the living Father has sent me, and as I live because of the Father, so he who eats me, he also shall live because of me. This is the bread that has come down from heaven; not as your fathers ate the manna, and died. He who eats this bread shall live forever. (John 6:56-59)*

In the last moments and in the last prayer before the solemn words of the actual consecration, we are struck anew by a wise and holy fear. There is a definite note of urgency in the request of this prayer: "Bless, consecrate, ratify, make reasonable and acceptable this bread." Emphasis is upon the overwhelming greatness of the change which is about to take place, as if to say, "Can it really be? Is it possible, is it reasonable to expect that this mere creature, bread, shall truly become the Body and Blood of the Son of God?" Here is the second mystery, the second unbelievable miracle. The first "sacrament" is the human nature of God-made-man. But now we are about to repeat the further miracle, the sacramental nature of God-made-man. Can it really be that such an immeasurable privilege is given us?

Yes—only with the blessing and approval of God, who has himself ordained and determined this mystery. It is not that we lack confidence in the power of God, or in his approval of what his Son, the head of the Church, is about to renew, since it was always the Father's plan to redeem man in this way. But we need to beware of becoming matter-of-fact, spoiled children, demanding or expecting or smugly taking for granted such a gift. If we truly appreciate what is to take place before us now, we quite naturally say over and over in our hearts, "Yes, Lord, give it your fullest blessing, for indeed we want and desire with all our energy that this bread may become your most sacred Body and Blood, but *you* must prepare the offering. We are in no way worthy or capable."

This beautiful Christian prayer of the Mass is venerable and ancient. It is already mentioned by St. Ambrose, in an earlier form, and in its present arrangement it dates back to Pope St. Gregory the Great (600 A.D.). With what a long-lived, noble, ancient, and universal family we pray, the ever-ancient, ever-modern family of Christ!

"Make this gift reasonable," we pray. The original form of this word (*rationabilis*) corresponds to the Greek word for spiritual, above the realm of matter, just as man's "rationality" or "reason" is above the material world. And indeed, the gift is now to rise, not only above matter, but above man himself, and above all God's creation, to the height of God himself.

And may we also rise with it, Lord, from the low depths of our material, earthbound apathy, from the low valley of our selfish schemes and empty plans, to the spiritual height on which we at last have something to offer, some sign of our love, our attention to you; may we "rise at last from sleep, because the Lord has raised us up," as the psalmist sings (Psalm 3:5). Climbing out of our befogged valley of sin, may we "ascend the mountain of God" with the newborn innocence of those "whose hearts are clean and whose desires are no longer vain" (Psalm 23).

In this connection we may take note of the five crosses or blessings which the priest during this prayer makes over the bread and wine, and the five corresponding crosses he makes in the prayer immediately following the consecration. The crosses, like the words with which they correspond, are symmetrically arranged "up to" and "down from" that solemn moment, like the ascent and descent of a mountain peak; the summit is ascended—where earth meets heaven—and the Son of God descends, taking over the substance of the bread and wine. . . .

1) bless † sanctify † approve † that it may become the Body † and Blood † of Jesus.

2) a sacrifice pure † holy † spotless, † the Bread of Life † and Cup of Salvation † .

*Prayer: Lord God of heaven's armies, Maker of all creation, you have led all that was nothingness into living reality; you have glorified our lowly nature by giving us power to dispense so sacred and beautiful and unspeakable a mystery. Be pleased with this sacrifice we present, Lord, and make it the sacrament of your only Son's Body and Blood.*

(*Offertory Prayer, Armenian Liturgy*)

# 35.

## HE IS HERE

On the day before he suffered, he took bread into his holy and venerable hands and with his eyes lifted up to you, his almighty Father in heaven, he gave thanks to you, he blessed it, broke it, and gave it to his disciples.

*For I myself have received from the Lord (what I also delivered to you), that the Lord Jesus, on the night in which he was betrayed, took bread, and giving thanks broke, and said, 'This is my body which shall be given up for you; do this in remembrance of me.' (1 Corinthians 11:23-24)*

The account of the most solemn moment at the Last Supper as given in the Missal does not appear in that exact form in any one of the evangelists. It is different from any of them, as they are different from one another. In this very difference of exact wording and in the very unity of meaning, we see the living Church in its growth and diversity, the living liturgies in their early variations and colorings, as the source from which the evangelists themselves drew their message.

Yet more is revealed upon close inspection. In these words of consecration we note that Jesus "lifted up his eyes to heaven," a recognizable symbol of offering it to his heavenly Father. This gesture is not recorded in the gospel accounts of the Last Supper, but in St. Matthew's account of the miracle of the five loaves with which Jesus fed five thousand men (Matt. 14:19). Thus the Church combines these scenes as Jesus himself did, to prepare the people for accepting the "bread of life." He had already indicated, then, his choice of bread by which to offer himself to the Father for the life of the world; he himself would be our food, "so that if any man eat of this bread, he will have life everlasting" (John 6:52).

And it is wise for us to see Jesus raising his eyes to heaven; it was to lift us up that he came down, and to lift us up he gave his flesh to be our bread, that we might have his life. We lift our eyes to heaven, too, for earth and heaven must meet here.

The words of consecration are "his words," rather than the Church's, or the priest's, or the people's. They are the priest's words, too, in a true sense, but it is really Jesus himself who acts now. Hence the actual words of consecration are, "This is My Body." It is Jesus speaking. And as he speaks, he is here, as he was when he said those words in the upper room. He is here in that bread, the same Jesus, the same offering, now in his glorified body, "He dies now no more." He lives among us, our pledge of future glory.

"He lifted his eyes to heaven, to you, his almighty Father." These words indicate the deep state of prayer of Jesus at this solemn moment, the perfect union of his will with his Father's. Such must be our state of mind at this moment. But a state of mind does not suddenly rush in, as though a vacuum were opened to it. It must arrive with preparation. Have our minds been prepared for such a union of wills?

*Prayer: Lord and loving master of all men, we unite our voices with the angelic spirits of heaven. We cry out: Holiness is yours; you are sacred above all things, you and your only-begotten Son and your Holy Spirit. You loved the world to such a degree that you gave us your only Son. He came to live in the world, and when he had accomplished everything that was planned for our redemption,*

*on the night during which he was betrayed, he took bread into his
holy, pure, and unblemished hands. He gave thanks, he blessed it,
making it holy, and he gave it to his holy disciples and apostles.*

(*Prayer of the Consecration, Greek Liturgy*)

# 36.

## THIS IS MY BODY

AND HE SAID: "TAKE AND EAT THIS, ALL OF YOU. FOR THIS IS MY
BODY."

*I am the living bread that has come down from heaven. If anyone*
*eat of this bread he shall live forever; and the bread that I will give*
*is my flesh for the life of the world. (John 6:51-52)*

How simple, how tremendous these words! The greatest actions
come with the least external show; how plain the visible shape of
events that have changed the course of history. The greatest virtues
seem the most effortless in execution, but what power and force
within!

"This is My Body." How many times have these stark, simple
words been heard in the midst of an overpowering silence, the
world's one moment of real reverence. Through twenty long centuries on our time-ravaged earth, these words have an eternal
youth, an unsullied purity, renewing the primitive shock of creation.

Like thousands of his countrymen, according to a tradition more
than a thousand years old, Jesus ate the Paschal Supper with his
twelve apostles. But there suddenly at the end of the meal, he kept
a promise made a year before—that he would be their sacrifice and
our sacrifice, since he was the living bread that came down from
heaven. He took unleavened bread into his hands, thanked his

heavenly Father for it, and declared, "This is My Body, given for you."

Who can count the times that it has been given to us since? Who can measure the joy it has given, the sorrow it has consoled, the strength it has provided, the love it has inspired? On the very day of his resurrection, two of his disciples recognized him in the renewal of this action, and in their joy they hastened from Emmaus back to Jerusalem to bring comfort to the saddened apostles. The first Christians at Jerusalem, after his ascension, "broke bread daily" in the gladness of their hearts, surrounded and persecuted as they were by enemies. Hunted, imprisoned, scourged, thrown to hungry lions, the heroic witnesses of Christ were comforted by this living bread. Driven underground by violence, they continued to celebrate the Eucharist at the very tombs of the martyrs who had shed blood before them. As the Church emerged, strong and purified, from the bloody purges, her children built churches in which to renew daily the offering of the living bread of heaven, and through its power drew the invading barbarians to the love of Christ.

Chapels of the poor were raised, medieval castles were sanctified by his presence, gigantic cathedrals were built—and there the Holy Sacrifice was offered, for the coronation of kings, for the funerals of popes and princes; for the victims of war, pestilence, and famine; to entreat the heavenly Father for good harvest, for long-awaited peace treaties, for the end of epidemics or the blessings of a jubilee. The living bread of the Eucharist became Christian man's greatest gift, for every solemn, sad, or joyous event; for the sanctification of marriages and coronations, religious vows and ordinations, and anniversaries and burials. The power of all emotions and all prayers and all hopes was now rolled into one: the white round of the sacred host. For to that bread he had spoken: "This is My Body."

*Prayer: He lived among us and among the human weaknesses of life, himself unspotted by any sin, and of his own free will he walked up to the Cross and accomplished redemption for us and for the whole world. He took bread into his holy, divine, innocent and venerable hands, blessed it, returned thanks, broke it, and gave it to his holy, chosen disciples who were at table with him. And he said, "This is My Body, which is given up for you and for the many, for the atonement and remission of sins."*

(*The Consecration, Armenian Liturgy*)

# 37.

## THIS IS MY BLOOD

SIMILARLY, AFTER HIS SUPPER, HE TOOK UP THIS EXCELLENT CHALICE INTO HIS HOLY AND VENERABLE HANDS. AGAIN HE GAVE THANKS TO YOU, BLESSED IT, AND GAVE IT TO HIS DISCIPLES, AS HE SAID, "TAKE AND DRINK THIS, ALL OF YOU. FOR THIS IS THE CHALICE OF MY BLOOD, OF THE NEW AND ETERNAL COVENANT, THE MYSTERY OF FAITH. IT SHALL BE SHED FOR YOU AND FOR MANY, TO ATONE FOR THEIR SINS."

*And taking a cup and giving thanks, he gave it to them, and they all drank it; and he said to them, 'This is my blood of the new covenant, which is being shed for many. Amen I say to you, that I will drink no more of the fruit of the vine, until that day when I shall drink it new in the kingdom of God.' (Mark 14:23-25)*

"He now took this most excellent chalice in his holy and venerable hands." These are words both of great love and great respect. The chalice and the hands that held it to give thanks are treated by the Church with careful reverence, a mark of true love—far from the cheap and worn "love" of popular usage, a selfish hankering for pleasure or company or admirers or flatterers. The only love worthy of its name is an intelligent and devoted respect which combines knowledge and understanding and appreciation and fear, which gives instead of taking, which listens rather than pouring out words.

There is in real love a trembling, a fear of doing harm or of

failure to see and to understand the sacredness of the beloved. Such
is the quality of the Church's love for her bridegroom, a model of
genuine love to inspire every Christian's love for Christ, to teach
all what "loving one another" means.

Redeemed, bought at a great price are we, saved by this most
excellent cup, the cup of incomprehensible suffering and self-
abandonment. . . . What respect, what fear of one another's souls
we ought to have! And yet how much of our prayer and sacrifice
and Mass-attendance has become empty ritual! We are slaves of
forms and traditions, performed "dutifully," with no relation to the
reality for which they must stand.

This is the sacrifice of Christ, who has given himself once for all
to save the world—its people, that is—from destruction. We are to
take part in that sacrifice here, in order to continue that part of ours
effectively in all else that we do.

But what do we accomplish, Lord? Is this tremendous action real
to us at all? Are we, day by day, hour by hour, truly and seriously
purifying ourselves to be worthy to offer and be offered with this
sacrifice? If it were so, would not the effect of our share in the Mass
be world-shaking? Would not our example be noticed? Would not
our interest in the work of God be inspiring and shocking? Would
it not awaken dead souls everywhere? What huge roadblocks we
throw between the power and its effect, between the gift and its
receivers, between the altar and those who should be attracted to it!

What do we really make of this miracle of the Mass, but a dreamy
or magic formula which we somehow expect to work of itself, with
little or no meaning for the rest of our lives? How do we really
apply the work of this sacrifice to living in the world with our
neighbors? But wasn't that the example of Christ—that the Last
Supper and Calvary were simply culminating expressions of what
his life had always been?

Are we right in insisting on a daily ritual of prayers and formulas
as though they alone by magic would make us holy? Can the mere
mumbling of ritual make the sacrifice of the Mass live in us? Is

the powerful life of grace which the Mass should effect in us really present?

These questions must continually trouble our consciences if we really intend to take our part in the Mass. It is our life-long duty to make the Mass real in ourselves.

*Prayer: Here, in truth, is the sacred Body of Jesus Christ, the Son of God. Amen. Here, most certainly, is the precious Blood of Jesus Christ, the Son of God. Amen. Here, in true reality, is the Body and Blood of Emmanuel, God of us all. Amen. I believe. Amen, amen, amen. I believe, I believe, I believe and will profess to my dying breath that here is the living Body Which your only-begotten Son, Jesus Christ our Master, our God, our Redeemer took from our Lady, Queen of all creation, the holy and immaculate Mary, virgin and mother of God. He united this Body to his divinity with confusion of mixture or change. He testified before Pontius Pilate, and himself he chose to be sentenced to the Cross for what we in fact deserved.*

(*Prayer before Communion, Coptic Liturgy*)

# 38.

## IN MEMORY OF ME

**WHENEVER YOU SHALL DO THESE THINGS, YOU SHALL DO THEM IN MEMORY OF ME.**

*In like manner he took also the cup, after he has supped, saying, 'This cup is the new covenant in my blood; do this as often as you drink it, in remembrance of me. For as often as you shall eat this bread and drink the cup, you proclaim the death of the Lord, until he comes.' (I Corinthians 11:25-26)*

Many of the ordinary, traditional, acceptable customs of both civilized and uncivilized peoples are done to keep alive the memory of those whom they love. We do many things to remember those we love most deeply, admire most completely, and respect most profoundly. Undoubtedly we limit our highest reverence to only a few most intimate and important people in our personal lives; we would need no customs or traditions to make us remember our most loved ones; it is a perfectly spontaneous and human gesture. Our parents, our spouse, our children and perhaps our very closest friend receive from us attention that is very like the veneration which the Church accords to saints.

We accord a kind of worship to those dearest to us: we desire to please them, we tend to imitate them—at least if they are somehow above us in rank—and our admiration tends to raise them ever higher. We listen to their every word, we form our own judgments

127

strongly upon their opinion, we seek their advice for every important decision, we are thrilled by their approval of our deeds, we are
deeply grieved by their expression of any displeasure at our actions.
We seek the company of these intimates whenever possible, we
remember them with frequent thought, letters, and the best choice
in gifts.

Most intimate of all friends, most reverenced, admired, and desired by every real Christian is Jesus Christ, Son of God and both
Father and Brother to us. Our most precious memories are of him,
his every word and movement, his every wish and advice, his
desires and his actions.

It is not surprising, then, that at this most sacred moment in the
renewal of Jesus' most important action, we, the Church, wish to
imitate him as men lost in awe and attention. With much reason
we see this precious minute of the Consecration not as a mere
memory or historical account; we see it as the living action of Jesus
himself. That is exactly what it is. "*Do* this in memory of Me," says
Jesus. So the priest in our name and with our wish takes the bread
into his hands (as Jesus did), lifts his eyes heavenward (as Jesus
did), bows as he gives thanks (as Jesus did), and blesses the bread,
as our Lord himself did. Later, in actions surrounding the Communion, the priest continues the work of Jesus in the detail of
"breaking the bread" and "giving it to his disciples to eat."

"As often as you do these things, you do them in memory of Me."
Jesus thus intended this banquet as a memorial, a reminder of him,
as well as an offering of himself for our cleansing. What takes
place before our eyes makes us *mindful* of him; we remember, we
overcome the weakness of forgetting him, we fill the emptiness of
our lives with his memory. The prayer which follows reiterates this
need—the need to remember Jesus always, in all that he is, in all
that he does, in all that he teaches and effects in us.

*Prayer: Do this in remembrance of me. As often as you eat this
holy mystery and drink this purifying blood, you announce my
death until I return again. We make memory of your death, Lord,*

*we proclaim your resurrection and we look for your second coming. We beg for your grace and forgiveness; we ask pardon for our sins. Let your mercy overshadow all of us. Remembering your great deed of salvation, O Christ, God of us all, we pray and request your goodness for that hour when you will return in majesty in the holy company of your angels, when you are robed in your beauty, when you demand of the earth that its tombs be opened, when the dead must rise and stand trembling before your judgment.*

(*Prayer after the Consecration, Syrian Liturgy*)

# 39.

## WE REMEMBER

NOW, LORD, WE YOUR SERVANTS UNITE WITH YOUR HOLY PEOPLE IN RECALLING THE HOLY SUFFERINGS OF THE SAME CHRIST, YOUR SON, OUR MASTER; WE REMEMBER HIS RESURRECTION FROM DEATH AND HIS GLORIOUS ASCENT TO HEAVEN. IN THIS RECOLLECTION WE OFFER TO YOUR SUBLIME MAJESTY, FROM THE GIFTS YOU HAVE GIVEN US, A PURE OFFERING, A HOLY OFFERING, A SPOTLESS OFFERING—THE SACRED BREAD OF ETERNAL LIFE AND THE CHALICE OF EVERLASTING REDEMPTION.

*And having taken bread, he gave thanks and broke, and gave it to them, saying, 'This is my body, which is being given for you; do this in remembrance of me.' In like manner he took also the cup after the supper, saying, 'This cup is the new covenant in my blood, which shall be shed for you. But behold, the hand of him who betrays me is with me on the table. For the Son of Man indeed goes his way, as it has been determined; yet woe to that man by whom he will be betrayed.' (Luke 22:19-22)*

The sacred Consecration of the bread and wine has been completed, as Jesus instructed us. Every word, every gesture, the intention and the reality has been renewed; the Lord's presence is assured, the Lord's own offering is repeated, the Lord's ransom is paid for us again. We have "done this in memory" of the Incarnate Son of God.

So now we *remember*, in the fullest sense of the word. St. Paul tells us that this bread and this cup, "the new covenant in his blood," is specifically a memorial of the Lord's death. "As often as you shall eat this bread and drink the cup, you proclaim the death of the Lord, until he comes. Therefore whoever eats this bread or drinks the cup of the Lord unworthily, will be guilty of the body and blood of the Lord."

But Jesus' death is an act of such glory that—as this prayer reminds us—we recall it always in connection with the glorious resurrection and ascension. It is a memorial of his life-giving death, a death intimately bound up with a transcendent new life, a death that opens the door and causes the new and greater life to be born. We desire to remember the suffering and resurrection of Jesus to such a degree that, in the penetrating words of St. Paul, "we carry this treasure" in our earthly minds and bodies, our "vessels of clay, to show that the greatness of our power is God's, not ours." We want never to forget this primary Christian action which has just been completed before our eyes, for as Christians we must always be "carrying about in our bodies the dying of Jesus, so that the life of Jesus may be made manifest in our mortal flesh" (II Corinthians 4:7, 10).

This deep, joyous paradox was already well known to the earliest Christians, as the quotation from St. Paul illustrates. Indeed, historians tell us that this majestic prayer of remembrance is one of the oldest in the liturgy, possibly going back as far as apostolic times. Surely its thought is rooted in the writings of the apostles.

This prayer is a beautiful parallel of the prayer at the end of the Offertory, "Accept, O Holy Trinity, this offering we make in memory of the Passion, Resurrection and Ascension of our Lord." Both texts indicate that these three actions of Jesus are inseparable and form one action, a unified plan and purpose. That plan is one with this offering, too, the "bread of eternal life and the chalice of redemption," a hint at the approaching Communion, the banquet that strengthens "your servants—the priests—and all your holy people."

*Prayer: Remembering this command which saved us and all the deeds which came into being for our sake—the cross and the burial, the resurrection after three days, the ascent to heaven to the throne on the right hand, the second glorious coming—we now offer to you what is your own, taken from what is your own, in all of us and for all of us. We adore you, we glorify you, we thank you, Lord, and we send up our worship to you, our God. We offer you this spiritual and unbloody sacrifice; we pray and ask and beg you to send your Holy Spirit into our hearts and upon our gifts.*

*(Prayer after the Consecration, Byzantine Liturgy)*

# 40.

## THE PERFECT SACRIFICE

BE PLEASED TO REGARD THESE OFFERINGS WITH A LOOK OF FAVOR AND APPROVAL; ACCEPT THEM AS YOU GRACIOUSLY ACCEPTED THE GIFTS OF YOUR UPRIGHT SERVANT, ABEL, THE OFFERING OF OUR FATHER, ABRAHAM, AND THE SACRIFICE OF YOUR GREAT PRIEST, MELCHISEDECH: A HOLY OFFERING, AN UNSPOTTED VICTIM.

*Abel also brought some of the firstlings of his flock with their fat portions. The Lord was pleased with Abel and his offerings; but for Cain and his offering he had no regard. (Genesis 4:4-5)*

*When Abram returned from the defeat of Chodorlahomor and the kings with him, the king of Sodom went out to meet Abram in the valley of Save—that is, in the king's valley. Then Melchisedec, the king of Salem, brought out bread and wine; for he was a priest of the Most High God. He blessed Abram and said, 'Blessed be Abram by the Most High God, creator of heaven and earth. Blessed be the Most High God, who has delivered your enemies into your hand.' Then Abram gave him a tenth of everything. (Genesis 14:17-20)*

The Church never forgets the Old Testament's connection with the new; the Old is the preparation, the foreshadowing, the beginning that grows into the New. So we recall the sacrifices of Abel, Abraham, and Melchisedech. Sacrifice goes with love, it grows with

*133*

love, it belongs with love; it is as old as history. But all history and all sacrifice were a preparation for this perfect one, for "the Law appoints as priests men who are weak; but the word of the oath, which came after the Law, appoints a Son who is forever perfect" (Hebrews 7:28).

This prayer is also one of the most ancient, founded solidly on the apostolic tradition, and clearly related to the Epistle to the Hebrews. The prayer refers to God's acceptance of Abel and Abraham, for their sacrifices were made with a pure heart. Our disposition is important: if only we were the perfect people that so perfect a sacrifice should inspire! Our unworthiness is frightful, when we consider what gift God has given us with which we may redeem ourselves.

Abel and Abraham are types of Christ. Abel was innocent and pleasing to God; Abel gave the best of his lambs, to prove that he gave the best of his love and reverence. How little of ourselves or our best are we willing to give! Abraham did not hesitate to offer his most precious treasure, as dear as his own life—his only son, his pride and his promise of future descendants, the "great nation" which God himself had promised Abraham. But if God so desired, Abraham did not complain of making that ultimate sacrifice. What are we willing to give, Lord, if anything at all? Can we utter this prayer with anything more than deepest shame?

For Abraham's thanksgiving, the mysterious Melchisedech offered bread and wine to the Lord. In this beautiful image, in this early prophecy, nearly two thousand years before the "breaking of the bread," the Lord indicated what the form of the perfect sacrifice was to be. Surely it is fitting to recall it here, as we see the priest now offering Jesus, the "holy and spotless victim," under the appearance of bread and wine.

All sacrifices ever offered to God are here fulfilled; all hopes of eventual perfection in man's offerings are here satisfied. In all ages holy men were, in a sense, Christian in virtue of that great hope which they felt—though perhaps they could not have defined it—

the hope of God's final revelation and man's full redemption, man's rescue from the threatening darkness.

*Prayer: Lord, our God, you accepted the sacrifice of Abel in the desert, of Noah when he came out of the ark, of Abraham when he ascended the mountain, of Elias on Mount Carmel, of David on the threshing-floor of Arauna the Jebusite, of the widow's mite in the temple; now receive favorably the offering and sacrifice which here is being presented to your holy name by your servant. Let it atone for his sins and the sins of all your people; be pleased to forgive him and them at this hour and in eternity, for all ages.*

*(The Preparation, Ethiopic Liturgy)*

# 41.

## OUR UNWORTHINESS

IN A HUMBLE SPIRIT WE ASK YOU, ALMIGHTY GOD, TO HAVE THESE
OFFERINGS CARRIED BY YOUR HOLY ANGEL TO YOUR HIGH ALTAR ABOVE,
IN THE PRESENCE OF YOUR DIVINE MAJESTY; THUS ALL OF US WHO
PARTAKE AT THIS ALTAR OF YOUR SON'S MOST SACRED BODY AND BLOOD
MAY BE FILLED WITH EVERY HEAVENLY GRACE AND BLESSING. THROUGH
THE SAME CHRIST OUR LORD. AMEN.

*And another angel came and stood before the altar, having a
golden censer; and there was given to him much incense, that he
might offer it with the prayers of all the saints upon the golden altar
which is before the throne. And with the prayers of the saints there
went up before God from the angel's hand the smoke of the incense.*
(*Apocalypse 8:3-4*)

"Bid these offerings be carried by your holy angel to your heavenly
altar." What nonsense for us to say this, when already on our
earthly altar—lowly as it is—we have the King of Angels himself!
But at this most solemn moment we are awestruck, and we babble
incoherently, it seems, like Peter on the mountain as Christ stands
transfigured before him: "Let us make three tabernacles here, Lord,
one for you, one for Moses and one for Elias." He is thunderstruck;
he simply does not know what to say. His plan may make little sense,

but it serves to express his overwhelming reverence and love and gratitude.

So our words now indicate our awe and our humility. This prayer, like the exclamation of Peter at the sight of Jesus' miraculous catch of fish on the Sea of Galilee, says, "Depart from me, Lord, for I am a sinful man." We beg that this most sublime and holy gift may be carried to the heaven of heavens by a holy messenger, for we are entirely unworthy. We feel like the prophet Isaias in the presence of God: "Woe is me, for I am a sinful man, born of a sinful race." And we stutter like Jeremias: "Ah, ah, ah, Lord, I cannot speak, for I am a mere child."

Thus our prayer, "command this spotless sacrifice to be carried off by a holy angel," is a prayer of helplessness in the face of the all-holy. "Lord, you are entirely too good for us; you should not have given us this offering; it is too far above what any of us have ever deserved. Yes, Lord, only your holy angels and your heavenly court can worthily bear this gift; nowhere ought anyone dare to look upon it; it should be seen only before the face of your divine majesty."

But we are not merely humbled at our unworthiness. We are not to be diffident and cowardly as Achaz the king who said out of a shallow, confused soul, "I will not ask a sign; I will not tempt the Lord my God." We indeed ask a sign, and ask to become worthy of receiving it. We have not begged to be delivered from what is too holy for us. We have asked it to rise above us because of our unworthiness, but only so that it might be sent back to us as a supreme gesture of God's mercy, whereby we who have stood at attention around this sacred altar, and have been bold enough to "receive the sacred Body and Blood of your Son, may be filled with every heavenly blessing and grace."

What a request, Lord! What a paradoxical prayer! Does it not make us wonder which of the two nearly opposite requests is more appropriate? Yet both are full of love and deep reverence. Is it not true that what we deeply love we always feel unworthy of, and yet we always find it painful to be separated from it?

*Prayer: In this holy mystery we stand in the place of the cherubim and chant the thrice-holy hymn to the Trinity, the giver of life; thus we must leave behind all worldly thoughts and cares. It is our high honor to welcome the King of the universe into our company, he the Lord who is carried on high on the invisible rapiers of holy angels in the armies of heaven! Alleluia, alleluia, alleluia! O God, cleanse me, a sinful man! Let our hands be raised to the service of heaven and let us praise the Lord!*

**(Prayer of the Great Entrance, Russian Eucharistic Liturgy)**

# 42.

## IN MEMORY OF THE DEPARTED

AND REMEMBER YOUR SERVANTS, LORD, [NAMES], WHO HAVE LEFT
THIS WORLD BEFORE US, BLESSED WITH THE SIGN OF FAITH, AND WHO
NOW REST IN THE SLEEP OF PEACE. [SPECIFIC REMEMBRANCES OF THE
FAITHFUL WHO HAVE DIED ARE MADE HERE.]

TO THESE, LORD, AND TO ALL WHO REST IN CHRIST, GRANT OUR
REQUEST FOR A PLACE OF REFRESHMENT, LIGHT, AND PEACE. THROUGH
THE SAME CHRIST OUR LORD. AMEN.

*And so betaking themselves to prayers, they besought him that
the sin which had been committed might be forgotten. But the most
valiant Judas exhorted the people to keep themselves from sin, foras-
much as they saw before their eyes what had happened, because of
the sins of those that were slain. And making a gathering, he sent
twelve thousand drachmas of silver to Jerusalem for sacrifice to be
offered for the sins of the dead, thinking well and religiously concerning the resurrection. (For if he had not hoped that they that
were slain should rise again, it would have seemed superfluous and
vain to pray for the dead.) And because he considered that they who
had fallen asleep with godliness, had great grace laid up for them,
it is therefore a holy and wholesome thought to pray for the dead,
that they may be loosed from sins. (II Machabees 12:42–46)*

Holy Mass is the spiritual banquet of God's family. True, the Mass as we know and celebrate it on earth is for God's earthly family, but since it is the Church's offering, the Church's gift and the Church's feast *par excellence,* and since it is Christ, the whole Christ and his Mystical Body making the gift, it concerns that whole body. That is why we did not forget the saints. For through Jesus Christ we are in constant communion with them; consequently at Mass we sit down to table with them. The same Lord who is their eternal banquet, their endless source of joy, is ours, too, at the Mass and most especially at the Mass.

Except for the Holy Eucharist itself, the perfect self-sacrifice of Jesus, the Church reminds us of nothing more frequently in the Mass than the Communion of Saints. At the opening confession of our faults we admitted our guilt before the saints and implored their special help. We ascended the altar, kissed it, and reminded the Lord of those "saints whose relics are here." In the Apostles' Creed we profess our faith in the Communion of Saints, and in the Nicene Creed we recall how the Holy Spirit "spoke through the prophets." At the final prayer of the Offertory we ask that the Holy Trinity receive our offering in memory of not only the life of Jesus, but of Mary, John the Baptist, the holy apostles and all the saints, that it may add "to their honor and our salvation." Most of the proper or common Masses of the year are celebrations of Saints' festal days, indicating our conviction that their joy is our joy, their victory is our victory, their holiness is in a sense our holiness, because they are members of our family, members in whom we take particular pride.

Among these holy ones of God we include the souls of our beloved dead. Their earthly journey is over; they are closer to God than we are. We have good reason to hope that they have sanctified their souls in the Blood of Jesus, as we are doing at this very Mass. They have passed the most serious test; they were found turned towards God. They need only perfect themselves now, burn out all imperfection, beautify their somewhat tarnished virtues, and they shall be ready for heaven. They are now what we hope to be

—holy souls suffering the last purification in that dark night experienced by the saints on earth. We are wise to offer them our spiritual aid, for they are in a good position to offer us theirs.

What better opportunity to return the gratitude we owe to so many of our departed benefactors? We failed to show them thanks and appreciation on earth. In God's mercy, we can still do so. We can still forgive, where we failed to on earth; we can still repair the harm we may have done, because the dead and the living are members of the one Body, and in it the dead live eternally. This Memento is surely the best we can give our beloved departed ones. What better thing could we do than to include them in the perfect offering of Jesus at the Mass? Far better than tears or flowers or tombstones, the Holy Sacrifice is a daily living remembrance that reaches them in eternity.

The Memento also expresses our hope for heaven, the place of "refreshment, light, and peace," our hope to join those for whom we express this best of all wishes. It is a kind of stepping stone into eternity, this Memento—a reminder of our own approaching end, as our list of remembered departed friends, relatives, co-workers, pupils, and parishioners grows ever greater.

*Prayer: Lord our God, grant a share in this sacrifice to our parents and relatives, our teachers and leaders, to our acquaintances who have died, and to all who have been and are in union with us in the celebration of these mysteries, those who have cooperated in building up the body of the Church from the day of her birth until the present day.*

(*Canon of the Mass, Maronite Liturgy*)

# 43.

## AND US SINNERS

We, too, your sinful servants, place our hope in your unlimited mercies; then graciously grant us a share and a bond
of friendship with your holy apostles and martyrs: with John,
Stephen, Matthias, Peter, Felicity, Perpetua, Agatha, Lucy,
Agnes, Cecilia, Anastasia, and all your saints. Admit us into
their company, not for the weight of our deserving deeds, but
for your generous forgiveness. Through Christ our Lord. Amen.

*You have come to Mount Sion, and to the city of the living God,
the heavenly Jerusalem, and to the company of many thousands of
angels, and to the Church of the firstborn who are enrolled in the
heavens, and to God, the judge of all, and to the spirits of the just
made perfect, and to Jesus, mediator of a new covenant, and to a
sprinkling of blood which speaks better than Abel. (Hebrews
12:22–24)*

To complete our remembrance of all the Body of Christ, we
must not forget the faithful on earth. Alas, Lord! Your "holy
people" are sinners, sometimes very great sinners, but they are
sinners with hope and with the desire to be perfected. For this
reason, at least, they are "your faithful."

We know that your real "faithful," who proved their fullness of
faith by a martyrdom of blood, or a martyrdom of unselfish living,

are the saints. We hope to be admitted into their company "not on our own merits" indeed, but out of your divine mercy. Still, we must be "tested as by fire" to be made worthy, even by the most indulgent mercy. Weak and cowardly as we are, dead God, fearful and thoughtful, we say with trembling, "Admit us into the company of your saints." Any Christian with the least understanding of his religion knows that making such a request is "asking for trouble," the trouble enjoyed by all of God's friends. If we, the members, are in any way to share the life of the head, Jesus Christ—if we, of his family, are in any way to resemble our eldest brother, the Man of Sorrows—we are somehow destined for crucifixion.

Chained as we are by our soft, weak flesh, we have the boldness of the Church thrust upon us, and how fortunate that is! Where we fail, the Church supports and strengthens us, so that at each Mass we are impelled to say, "Let us join the company of the saints, Lord. You alone can make us worthy, but we alone—by the free will you allow—can ask you to send us this 'trouble.'"

"We ask you, give us a share and deep friendship with the saints." How much to meditate here! What will this sharing in the lot of the saints mean? What makes them saints? The "trouble" we have been suggesting—and that is a paradoxical trouble. It is easy to misunderstand it, to have a wrong, gloomy, Nordic notion of self-abasement—thinking nothing of self, the destruction of pride. But it is not self-destruction that sanctifies; in itself obliteration of pride leaves a vacuum.

Is it not rather "overwhelming realization" that makes a saint? Vainglory does not make a saint—true. But for a saint glory is never in vain. It floods the heart. "Yes, indeed I know that God has favored me, far above nearly all the rest of the world. He has blessed me, materially, intellectually, spiritually above millions of my own countrymen. What God has given me is the very best," says the saint. "I know it well. My life takes its spur and its hope and its energy from that knowledge, a real knowledge, the deep experience of God's favor. But all this is owing to no merit of my own; it is God's work, from the very moment of my conception, from my baptism, my Communions, my high vocation in life, my un-speakable privileges as a Christian. He has poured the best ointment on me; I want to give him the best in return. All else, anything less is unworthy of manly gratitude."

*Prayer: In compliance with your commandment, we are now assembled, we, your feeble, wayward, unprofitable servants, for you have brought grace to life within us in marvelous fashion beyond our power to repay; you clothed yourself in our human nature in order to bring us life from your divine nature; you gave dignity to our lowly state and lifted us from our fallen state; you restored life to our deathly state and brought redemption from our slavery to sin; you brought light to our minds and defeat to our enemies, O Lord our God. You brought strength to our feeble, fragile nature through the overflowing kindness of your grace.*

**(Prayer after the Consecration, Chaldean Eucharistic Liturgy)**

# 44·

## ALL IS BLESSED

THROUGH HIM YOU ARE ALWAYS CREATING, SANCTIFYING, GIVING
LIFE, BLESSING AND AWARDING US ALL THESE GOOD GIFTS.

*He is the image of the invisible God, the firstborn of every
creature. For in him were created all things in the heavens and on
the earth, things visible and things invisible. . . . All things have
been created through and unto him, and he is before all creatures,
and in him all things hold together. (Colossians 1:15–17)*

This prayer was once a blessing of all the foods and offerings
brought to the altar by the faithful. We may say that it is still a
blessing of all we offer, since it blesses all created things.

All things on earth were blessed, made holy when God became
man on earth, when God redeemed his fallen creation by his own
most sacred presence. All nature was glorified and supernaturalized
when his most holy shadow passed over it.

Hence the blessing of the Sacrifice of Jesus is here extended to all
creation—not only ourselves, but all earthly things, our homes, the
works of art in them (let us hope there are some good ones!),
our land, our food, our work, our talents, our thoughts, and our
plans. They are all sanctified in him, in his abiding presence, and
in his renewal of the earth by the act of redemption. We are sanctified in him most of all, and we are blessed in all creation and can be

sanctified through it. The Holy Mass is the action of religious men, God's "holy nation," and holy men see the person of God behind and in all things. Just as the Lord said to Abraham of the Redeemer, "In your seed all the nations of the earth shall be blessed," so we say, "In the shadow of Jesus the Restorer, all creatures on earth are blessed."

This beautiful lesson was taught repeatedly in the Old Testament and frequently renewed in the New. The voice of God in all its power was heard by the psalmist towering above the cedars, splitting them in the majesty of the storm, thundering over vast waters, twisting giant oak trees, stripping forests and making the very mountains tremble.

As the might of God was seen through the awesome movements of his creatures, so the tender care and concern of God for his least children was seen by the Son of Man in the glory enjoyed by the lilies of the field, the food provided for the birds of the air, and the very hairs of our head, which our Lord assured us were "all numbered" by the Almighty Father.

His power, his care, and his blessing, then, extend to all things, and all are renewed in his saving power. The "very high mountains leap like young lambs" in the presence of the total offering of "the Lamb of God," who on the cross and on the "altar of sacrifice" takes away the sins of the world and brings the blessing of a new sanctity. "The earth is the fruit of God's work," the psalmist assures us, in reference to the original acts of creation. Should the earth not be the "fruit of God's work" anew in the sublime act of redemption and renewal?

*Prayer: Let us lift our voices in prayer to the Lord; Lord, show us your mercy. For the precious gifts that have become our offering, let us pray, that God out of his love for humankind may accept them on the holy altar of mystery; let us raise our voices in prayer to the Lord. That he may spare us the wrath of his judgment, let us pray to the Lord. In your keeping, most high God, we place all our life and all our hope; prepare us to share fittingly in the divine mysteries of your sacred banquet.*

(*Preface to the Communion Litany,
Russian Liturgy*)

# 45.

## THROUGH HIM AND WITH HIM

THROUGH HIM AND WITH HIM AND IN HIM IS GIVEN TO YOU, GOD, ALMIGHTY FATHER, IN UNION WITH THE HOLY SPIRIT, ALL HONOR AND GLORY, FOR ALL AGES OF THE WORLD. AMEN.

*For it has pleased God the Father that in him all his fullness should dwell, and that through him he should reconcile to himself all things, whether on the earth or in the heavens, making peace through the blood of his cross. (Colossians 1:19–20)*

In this final prayer of the Canon, much is contained. It is a climax of praise, a burst of joy over the glory that is Christ's, and all the world's, in Christ. The priest here lifts up the offerings, the bread and wine, now become the great sacrament, the living bread, Jesus Christ, perfect offering to God for man. By raising this sublime gift upward to God, we offer with it the whole created universe. All is elevated to God the Father through Christ our Lord.

At the Offertory we recalled how wonderfully God has taken part in our nature by becoming man, and we prayed that we might strive to become partakers in his divinity, since he condescended to partake of our humanity. He, God and man, is the bridge, then, between heaven and earth, drawing earth up to heaven. So whatever glory is lifted heavenward from all that we do which is noble and generous and selfless, whatever beauty there is in our devoted love to spouse and family, to friend and neighbor, whatever forgiveness we have for enemy and persecutor, whatever poverty we practice, whatever privation we endure, whatever labors we undergo in the service of our fellowman, all good is taken up to God through Jesus Christ, the bridge.

If we have the gift of persuasion with which to convince our fellowmen by our speech, if we have a personality to attract them to our way of life, if we have intelligence with which to teach and inspire them, if we have the gift of humor with which to bring laughter and humility into their lives, if we have sympathy with which to share their burdens—all these talents are brought to honor and glory through him—and only through him, with him—and with no other—and in him, for he is the cause and consequence of all goodness.

All honor and glory on earth, as all honor and glory in heaven, is through Jesus, the universal mediator; it is with Jesus, united with him, the "firstborn of all creation, in whom all completeness dwells. . . , who alone restores all things, making peace on earth and in heaven by his blood," and in him, in the oneness of the Mystical Body, that we have real value. He is the vine, we are the branches; without him we are dead, we "can do nothing."

Christ Jesus is our life, life with God and life with each other and life within ourselves. To this great reality we utter a final round of praise at the end of the sacred canon, as we stand united around his table, offering ourselves at his altar of sacrifice, and sharing his life in the unique intimacy of the Mystical Body.

The fullness of this life is the Christian's greatest earthly desire. Amen—so be it—our one true hope!

*Prayer: O Sovereign Lord, all-powerful God, Father of our God and Master and Redeemer Jesus Christ, we thank you for all creation and in all creation and through all creation; for you have defended and strengthened us, you have redeemed us to yourself, you have pitied us and led us safely to this moment.*

*(Preparation Prayers, Coptic Liturgy)*

# 46.

## OUR FATHER

LET US PRAY: INSTRUCTED BY OUR SAVIOR'S REDEEMING MESSAGE AND
FORMED BY HIS DIVINE TEACHING, WE ARE CONFIDENT TO SAY: OUR
FATHER WHO ARE IN HEAVEN. . . .

*And it came to pass as he was praying in a certain place, that
when he ceased, one of his disciples said to him. 'Lord teach us to
pray, even as John also taught his disciples.' And he said to them,
'When you pray, say: Father, hallowed be thy name. Thy kingdom
come! Give us this day our daily bread, and forgive us our sins,
for we also forgive everyone who is indebted to us. And lead us not
into temptation.' (Luke 11:1-4)*

The rite of Holy Communion begins. We are soon to be united
to Jesus Christ in the Eucharistic sacrament. The emphasis in Holy
Communion, as in our daily life itself, must always be on Christ,
not on ourselves. We were created to carry out his will, not our
own. His is the infinite wisdom, not ours.

So it is most fitting that we begin this part of the Mass with his
words, and not our own. We have come here to raise ourselves up
to God, rather than to bring him down to us; we must become
partakers with him, if Holy Communion is to improve us and
transform us, if it is to be a fruitful meeting between man and God,
if it is to be a true union at all.

150

Behold with what loving words he teaches us to pray. What unspeakable favors of God to men are revealed by these words of Jesus! When we consider God's excellence compared with ours, we must of necessity be thunderstruck by the words of the *Our Father*. He teaches us to call him "our Father." He adopts us as his sons, he makes us members of his family. "Urged by our Savior's command and formed by his divine schooling, we dare to say: Our Father." How would we have the courage and bravado otherwise? It is surely no right of ours by nature or inheritance or merit. No, it is only his overwhelming mercy. The lavish privileges announced and implied by the tender words of the *Our Father* could not be ours to believe or accept unless by the divine promises.

"Give us this day our daily bread." Like every good father, and indeed, more than the best of earthly fathers, the heavenly Father feeds us, nourishes us, clothes us, and gives us a home. These things he has provided for us on earth by the very nature of his creation; it is only when man's injustice interferes, when man refuses to imitate the charity of the heavenly Father, that these gifts are denied to many. That is why the Son of God warned us that we must "seek first the kingdom of God and his justice," and all else would be given us besides.

Greater than earthly bread is provided us. Our heavenly Father has provided heavenly food, the bread of life for our spiritual growth in grace; he has clothed us with a supernatural glory entirely above our greatest dreams of beauty and dignity; he has given us a home in the fullest sense: for we know that "we have here on earth no lasting home; ours is a heavenly city in the world to come" (Hebrews 13:15).

What a joy, what an unparalleled privilege to speak to such a Father, at the beginning of that part of the Mass in which the banquet is spread for us, his children.

*Prayer: We give thanks to you, O King invisible, because you created the universe in your unsearchable might and strength; you brought all things into being from emptiness, through the force of your overflowing charity. O Lord most high, look kindly from heaven on those who have worshipped your majesty. . . . Through the merits and the mercy of your only Son. . . . Lord Jesus Christ, our God, you are seated at the right hand of the Father and, though unseen, you are present here with us. With the power of your own hand, give us the gift of your most sacred Body and your most holy Blood.*

(*Prayer after the* Our *Father,* Russian Liturgy)

# 47.

## DELIVER US

DELIVER US, GRACIOUS LORD, FROM ALL EVILS, PAST, PRESENT AND FUTURE; BY THE INTERCESSION OF BLESSED AND GLORIOUS MARY, EVER VIRGIN, MOTHER OF GOD, OF THE BLESSED APOSTLES PETER AND PAUL AND ANDREW AND ALL SAINTS, MERCIFULLY GRANT PEACE IN OUR TIME; THEN THROUGH THE SUPPORT OF YOUR GENEROUS MERCY, WE MAY REMAIN ALWAYS FREE OF SIN AND SAFE FROM DISTURBANCES. THROUGH THE SAME JESUS CHRIST YOUR SON OUR LORD, WHO LIVES AND RULES, GOD, IN UNITY WITH THE HOLY SPIRIT, WORLD WITHOUT END. AMEN.

*Deliver me, O Lord, from evil men; preserve me from violent men, from those who devise evil in their hearts, and stir up wars every day. (Psalm 139:2)*

*And may the peace of God which surpasses all understanding guard your hearts and your minds in Christ Jesus. For the rest, brethren, whatever things are true, whatever honorable, whatever just, whatever holy, whatever lovable, whatever of good repute, if there be any virtue, if anything worthy of praise, think upon these things. (Philippians 4:7-8)*

This urgent petition is a continuation of the last request of the *Our Father:* "save us from evil." The only fear, the only failure, the only tragedy is in the human heart. All is good, all is well with us, all is joy and growth and profit and eternal promise, if only the human heart within us is untainted, uncorrupted, unselfish, unspoiled.

Evil is all around us in material forms—cold, hunger, want, disease, physical injury, pain, slow death or sudden death. But none of this can harm us if our hearts are pure. In recognition of this fact, the Church prays during Lent, "Protect your people, Lord, and in your mercy wash away their sins. For if they harbor no wickedness, no evil shall hurt them." No enemy has the power to conquer an uncorrupted heart. From that one evil, Lord, "past, present, or future," deliver us. For it has merited damnation for some in the past, it is our one danger in the present, it would destroy the grace that is our one promise for the future.

With the help of all the heavenly court, grant, O Lord, peace in our days. Here the great series of petitions for *peace* begins. We ask so often for that gift during the communion part of the Mass. What is that peace which we have heard in the Gloria, which we requested for the souls of the departed, which we beg for now and in the *Pax Domini,* the *Agnus Dei,* and in that beautiful prayer for peace which follows it, the first of the three Communion prayers?

What peace? Freedom from war—guns, bombs, conquest, captivity? Hardly—or else might we not say with some bitterness that the prayer has never been heard? We have seldom had such peace before or after Christ. But Jesus said, "*My* peace I give to you." Did *he* enjoy such peace—freedom from enemies, from treacherous plots, from murderous betrayal and torture to death at the hands of haters? No, throughout his public life he could say truthfully, "I have not come to bring peace but the sword." He had come, we might say, to arm his followers for battle!

During these communion prayers, then, we must meditate on this *peace,* to see what Jesus meant by it, for clearly the Church means to make it prominent and emphatic by its frequent repetition. We cannot afford to misunderstand the word.

Pilate asked, "What is truth?" but inquired no further. We ask, "What is peace?" but we must seek it. The psalmist advised, "Search for peace and pursue it." Where shall we search for it, and where shall we expect to find it?

*Prayer: Lord, receive our kind and reverent memento of the Virgin Mary, mother of God, of the saintly fathers who found favor with you in celebrating the memorial of the Savior's body and blood; we also offer it on your holy altar as you instructed us. Give pervading peace and serenity to the world, so all men may learn that you are their God, the living Father who sent them your dearly loved Son, Jesus Christ our Lord.*

*(Prayers before the Consecration, Liturgy of Malabar)*

# 48.

## BREAKING OF THE BREAD

THE PEACE OF THE LORD BE ALWAYS WITH YOU. AND WITH YOUR SPIRIT.

*And they continued steadfastly in the teaching of the apostles and in the communion of the breaking of the bread and in the prayers. (Acts 2:42)*

In the time of Christ large loaves were baked, whether of leavened or unleavened bread. The "breaking of bread" was a term especially applied to the taking of an important meal, a final banquet with friends on an occasion of special significance. At Emmaus the disciples "knew Jesus in the breaking of the bread." This, the Evangelists and St. Paul tell us, was done at the Last Supper by Jesus in the institution of the sacrament; he "broke it and gave it to his disciples."

The breaking of the bread as we now have it in the Mass is symbolic of our sharing in Christ. We have asked in the previous prayer that we might be freed from all sins and the turbulence of mind that weakens us and leads us to sin. The bread is broken for us so that we might take a part of it. This was the original purpose of breaking the large round loaves. In fact the bread is still broken for us, into the small round hosts, the part that we receive, and that is symbolically our part with Christ. It is also our part with each other in the Mystical Body.

Our part with each other—symbolized in the breaking of the bread—is a "hard saying" for many Christians, but a necessary one, if we are to be Christians at all. Our disagreements with others are often superficial and even childish; yet they cause many unkind attitudes and actions, and too often downright harsh and cruel treatment of others. How much of our spite and revenge is the product of an immature mind, if not an idiotic one. How important, then, to our small, prejudiced minds is this unvarnished truth thrust at us in "the breaking of the bread"—we are part of one another because we take part in the same Christ, offered for us in the one same sacrifice! If our minds are not broad enough or not large enough to listen to the opinions of our fellowmen and bear their weaknesses, let our minds and wills at least be kind enough to forgive.

"You will know the truth," said Jesus, "and the truth will set you free." Free, because we will no longer be slaves to every petty offense and every small disquieting difference. If the saints could pray for their cruel pagan persecutors with true love, can we not at least be tolerant of our fellow Christians?

This thought of union with our brother Christians at Mass is one element, surely, of the "peace of the Lord" which the priest wishes us at this point. This holy greeting is given us at every Mass, and at solemn Mass the kiss of peace is added to it. It would be a meaningful ceremony at every Mass, lest we forget our purpose here on earth. One reason for partaking in the Mass with our neighbors is surely to fulfill an obligation to one another in the Mystical Body, and to be reminded of the other duties of our membership in that body.

*Prayer: O Christ, you are the peace that permeates heaven and the one hope of all who are on earth; bring the peace and order which you give to the four ends of the earth, in particular to the holy Church universal, and to the harmony of church and state. Wipe out war throughout the world, scatter those whose desire is bloody conquest; thus may we live in confidence and thoughtfulness and the fear of God. Not to us, Lord, not to us the glory; let your name alone be glorified.*

*(Prayer for Peace, Liturgy of Malabar)*

# 49.

## LAMB OF GOD

LAMB OF GOD, WHO TAKES AWAY THE SINS OF THE WORLD, HAVE
MERCY ON US. . . . GRANT US PEACE.

*The next day John saw Jesus coming to him, and he said, 'Behold
the lamb of God, who takes away the sins of the world! This is
he of whom I said: After me there comes one who has been set
above me, because he was before me.' (John 1:29–30)*

These were John the Baptist's words of introduction to Jesus.
Would not the Jews who heard him have thought of the Paschal
Lamb? What a world of symbolic meaning and deep thoughts
John opened when he gave this name to the Messiah! We who
study modern poetry or literary forms of any kind ought to appreciate the wealth of meaning in the symbol of the Lamb who
takes away the world's sins. The very phrasing is a paradox. A lamb
usually tends to suggest innocence and gentleness and lovableness,
and these meanings do apply to the Lamb of God. But although he
is a sacrificed victim, there is really nothing helpless about him; he
goes of his own free will, and by men's outrage upon him he effects
a mighty cleansing. The tender young lamb, so apparently harmless
and powerless, is the most powerful force in the world!

Here is a lamb of gigantic proportions! Here is an explosive
symbol, worthy of the greatest prophets, the greatest revolutionists,

the greatest leaders! There are many, O Lamb of God, who would like to purge the world of all evil, all sin and its horrible effects. But how many would have the humility or self-control to do it with the meekness, the silence, the self-effacement of a *lamb*? What a tremendous union of tenderness and power is this lamb, worthy indeed of God!

What power, what love, what grief, what chastening humility this cry to the Lamb of God should evoke in every Christian soul!

"Lamb of God, cleansing the world of sin, grant us peace." When the Lamb of God was born in the cave of Bethlehem, angels appeared, singing glory to God and promising peace on earth to men of good will. What peace were men of good will to enjoy? Freedom from persecution or enemies or false friends or betrayals or abandonment? What nation on earth however Christian, however good its will, or what saint has ever enjoyed such peace since the night it was promised? And did not the very Lord in whose name peace was promised, predict that "nation shall rise up against nation, and kingdom against kingdom, and there will be pestilences and famines and earthquakes in various places. But all these things are the beginnings of sorrows"? And to his saints he added, "Then they will deliver you up to tribulation, and will put you to death; and you will be hated by all nations for my name's sake. And then many will fall away, and will betray one another, and will hate one another. And many false prophets will arise and will lead many astray. And because iniquity will abound, the charity of the many will grow cold" (Matthew 24:7–12).

What peace, then? Personal calm and quiet "in a good home" with a "good wife or husband," with "well-adjusted children" gurgling and cooing contentment? A life of ease and security without struggle or hardship? The ancient Hebrew concept of peace seemed almost to imply this kind of material affluence and calm. But was this the promise of Christ, who said, "The time is coming when those who kill you will think they are doing a service to God"? Does not the Lamb of God signify cleansing through sacrifice and slaughter?

*Prayer: O Lord Jesus Christ, come to us to make us holy; give us your most sacred body and your most glorious blood. Let us contemplate: what is holy is for the holy! One only is holy: one is Lord of all, Jesus Christ. The Lamb of God is broken and given to us—broken but not separated into parts, eaten but not destroyed, bringing sanctity to all who are nourished by it.*

(*Prayer before Communion, Ruthenian Liturgy*)

# 50.

## PEACE I LEAVE YOU

LORD JESUS CHRIST, YOU SAID TO YOUR APOSTLES, "PEACE I LEAVE YOU, MY PEACE I GIVE YOU." TAKE NO NOTICE OF MY SINS, BUT OF THE FAITH OF YOUR CHURCH. IN YOUR GOODNESS GRANT PEACE TO HER AND UNITY TO ALL IN HER, ACCORDING TO THE WISDOM OF YOUR WILL; FOR YOU ARE THE LIVING AND REIGNING GOD FOR ALL THE AGES OF ETERNITY. AMEN.

*Peace I leave with you, my peace I give to you; not as the world gives do I give to you. Do not let your heart be troubled, or be afraid. (John 14:27)*

This prayer, culmination of the successive requests for peace, holds the key to understanding that peace. For in it we remind Jesus, "Lord, you said to your apostles, peace I leave you, *my* peace I give you." And when you said so, Lord, you added, "*Not* as the world gives do I give peace to you."

So the peace that Christ promised was not at all the peace understood by the world. No, the Son of God himself, perfect man that he was, entirely spotless and free from sin as he was, Savior and Redeemer that he was, never enjoyed such peace. He was hated, envied, criticized, slandered. Throughout his public life those religious leaders who should have been his strongest supporters were trying to trap him and have him executed for alleged crimes.

What peace was yours, Jesus? You found no peace as the world gives even in the seclusion of your small home town. Those who should have known and loved you most personally turned against you; the mob tried to lynch you, to stone you and throw you head-long from a cliff near your own home. You, the Prince of Peace, never experienced worldly peace. No, even in your infancy you had to flee your native country; they left you no peace.

How, then, dare we ask you for this blessing? Only because you insisted that we share your peace. What was your peace—as your apostles brought you the news that Herod "the fox" sought to do away with you? What was your peace—when you asked the Phari-sees, "Why do you seek to kill me?" What peace did you enjoy— as they picked up stones to cast at you and you hid yourself and left the temple? What peace did you know—as you informed your twelve closest friends that one of them was on the verge of betraying you? In what realm of peace was your soul comforted—when for the third time you predicted that you would be handed over to the Gentiles to be scourged and mocked and spit upon and put to death? By what pact of peace had your own chosen people rejected you?

The one peace which your every word and gesture bespoke was the perfect peace of being one in purpose with your heavenly Father. This was your peace—not as the world gives it—the peace of a perfect conscience, the peace of unity with your Father's will, the peace of an unspotted love. We understand to some extent what you meant by your peace, Jesus, when we speak of "making our peace with God." By that we mean freeing ourselves of all selfish rebelliousness and restoring our errant wills at last to union with God's will.

There indeed is the only true peace, understood clearly by Dante when in his Paradiso he exclaimed, "In His Will is our peace." God's friends have peace. If we refuse to submit to that loving divine will, there is no peace. Life is a perpetual war until we surrender to God, for peace comes only from him. That is why the world is constantly at war, enjoying no peace: because it resists God. Job knew, as we must know, that "no man has resisted God and had peace!"

*Prayer: O generous and transcendent God, you have prepared a blessed table of spiritual strength for us, through your only-begotten Son, our Lord, our God and Redeemer, Jesus Christ. In your mercy, receive our unbloody sacrifice. Send us, Lord, the gifts of the Holy Spirit; grant us worthiness to come near your Holy of Holies with a clean heart and an upright conscience. Grant us the same peace which your beloved Son granted to his blessed disciples. As we give the holy kiss of peace to one another, we praise your goodness, almighty Father; we praise your only Son and your Holy Spirit, who creates life and who is worshipped in union with you, at this present moment and for all time and for the ages of ages forever. Amen.*

(*Prayer for Peace, Malankarese Eucharistic Liturgy*)

# 51.

## SEPARATE ME NOT

Lord Jesus Christ, Son of the living God, by your Father's will and in union with the Holy Spirit, you brought the world to life through your death. By your most sacred body and blood, rescue me from all my iniquities and from every kind of evil. Make me ever faithful to your commandments, and do not allow me to separate myself from you. With the same God the Father and the Holy Spirit, you are the living and governing God forever and ever. Amen.

*If you love me, keep my commandments. And I will ask the Father and he will give you another Advocate to dwell with you forever, the Spirit of Truth whom the world cannot receive, because it neither sees him nor knows him. But you shall know him, because he will dwell with you, and be in you. I will not leave you orphans; I will come to you. . . . In that day you will know that I am in my Father, and you in me, and I in you. (John 14:15-20)*

"You gave life to the world by your death." You found no better way; there were easier ways, but not ways of perfect love. What love was more complete? What love was more likely to convince us in spite of our ungrateful nature that your care for us was permanent and immovable? No, not death itself could shake your love for us.

The true lover will suffer all things for those he loves. Yet, if possible, he does not want to be separated from those he loves. He accepts all sacrifices for them, but since he loves them, he wants to be with them, to bring them more joy, to soothe their pains, to hear their desires and complaints, to attend to their daily needs. He wants to be with them in order to bring them happiness, ever when they least appreciate him.

All these signs of true love are exemplified most perfectly in you, Lord Jesus. You have rescued us at the greatest price, that of the most painful death, after a life spent teaching us the mysterious way to happiness. For those with the good will to listen, you unlocked the secret of peace amidst the greatest trials and sufferings. You died to insure us of the strength to pursue true peace. Then you provided us with your holy Body and Blood, the very sacrifice by which your love for us was proven, and your joy was shared with us.

It is for us to avail ourselves of this infinitely rich gift. If we love you, we are most eager to use this sacrament, our opportunity to be near you, and to receive your pledge of future glory. So "by this, your most holy Body and Blood, deliver me from all my sins and from all evils." Burn away the ugly sores of my imperfect love by the purging fire of your most pure love.

Then bring me strength and peace, Lord, through the power I possess when I "cling to your commandments." In your will my love is true and my peace is permanent. And never let me be separated from you again, for I cannot live in such a state. Lord God, you are too great; no one can escape from you. We can escape from a human enemy—to another town, another state, another country, if we are fortunate. Soon, perhaps, to another planet! Many have attempted to escape tyrants; happy those who escaped; tragic those who failed!

But from God, who can escape and who is such a fool as to desire escape? Who but a frightfully twisted soul wants to escape perfect love? Who cannot submit to being loved purely and sincerely, but only he who does not know how to love purely and sincerely in return?

*Prayer: Lord God, it is not right that you should make your abode under the roof of my soiled house; I have merited your wrath by the evil I have done before you; I have stained my soul and body, and I have neglected what is good. But by the human nature you assumed for my benefit, by your victorious death on the cross and your resurrection on the third day, I beg your pardon for the sins I have committed.*

**(Prayer before Communion, Ethiopic Liturgy)**

# 52.

## A HEALING REMEDY

Unworthy as i am, i venture to receive your body, Lord Jesus Christ; let it not lead to a judgment of condemnation against me. Because of your gracious goodness let it be a healing remedy for soul and body, as you live and reign with God the Father and with the Holy Spirit, one God forever and ever. Amen.

*Therefore whoever eats this bread or drinks the cup of the Lord unworthily, will be guilty of the body and blood of the Lord. But let a man prove himself, and so let him eat of that bread and drink of the cup; for he who eats and drinks unworthily, without distinguishing the body, eats and drinks judgment to himself. (I Corinthians 11:27-29)*

"Time heals all wounds," an old sage once said. He may have been old, but he was not wise, for this proverb is not true. Time heals nothing; it may infect and corrupt and rot and kill as well as heal. It is not time that heals; it is response.

Physical healing takes place only if the body responds effectively to the wound. The body must heal by the full, balanced use of its counteractive powers. Likewise, mental healing takes place only if the mind responds sufficiently to the wound. The mind must heal its wounds by the full use of its counteractive ability. That power

in the human mind is the power of intellect and will, recognition
and love.

That is why we pray with fear, Lord, that our mind and body be
receptive to your great healing remedy. For if we do not respond, we
shall only be further corrupted by your sacred presence within us—
horrible thought! Alas! Love must meet love; true love must meet
true love; holy and divine love must meet holy and divine love, or
there can be no remedy and no healing.

Must we fear to approach the sacred table, then, because of our
unworthiness? How does corruption dare to associate with pure
love? This is no mere oratory; it is the reality. Every sin, every evil
tendency, every neglect of the divine will, every idle thought makes
us unworthy of his sacred presence. If God means anything real
to us, then surely he is the One—and absolutely the only One—
Love that demands our total and complete surrender. Any lesser love
that would draw us away from him is a desecration of the most
noble power we possess. What is greater in man than that sacred
force which moves him to love his Creator, to find in God the
source of all goodness and beauty, to respond to the infinitely pure
love?

Is it presumption, then, for us to approach the most Holy One?
Of course it is! All the fear and trembling which comes with the
recognition of one's presumption is a necessary sentiment; it must
accompany us to the communion table. If we are to talk of sentiment, how much greater than the power of all human sentiment is
this gift of God! But those who receive it are human, possessing
human sentiments.

Is not all great love possessed with fear and trembling, with
inconceivable awe and wonder, with deep feelings of unworthiness?
Does not a true lover worry—in a glorious sense? Does he not
unconsciously examine himself to see wherein he may fail to give
true attention and service to his beloved? Do not some of the
greatest love tragedies in literature and history grow out of the
lovers' true (if perhaps exaggerated) sense of his unworthiness, out
of the lover's excessive grief over some failure of his? If sentiments

less than these accompany us to the table of union with God, it is because we do not fully realize what we are about to do. That is why we must pray with the priest and with our fellow-Christians that this sacrament may be "the healing remedy" we desperately need.

*Prayer: For all who partake of it, may the Body and Blood of Christ be the assurance and the promise of life in the world to come, of atonement for sins, of new strength for body and soul, of new light for the spirit, of defence at the awesome judgment-throne of Christ, the Anointed One. Let none of your holy people be doomed, Lord. Make us fitting partakers in your joy, rather, in your divine eternal, vivifying mysteries. Amen.*

**(Prayer of the Epiclesis, Malankarese Liturgy)**

# 53·

## I WILL TAKE IT

I WILL TAKE THE BREAD OF HEAVEN, AND I WILL CALL ON THE NAME OF THE LORD.

*Jesus then said to them, 'Amen, amen, I say to you, Moses did not give you the bread from heaven, but my Father gives you the true bread from heaven. For the bread of God is that which comes down from heaven and gives life to the world. . . . I am the bread of life. He who comes to me shall not hunger, and he who believes in me shall never thirst.' (John 6:32–35)*

Though I am most certainly unworthy of the gift, I would be even more unworthy if I refused it. Lord, this is the dilemma in which I find myself at this solemn moment. First I want to say to you, like Peter, "Lord, you shall never wash my feet." For this sacramental act of yours is surely as great a humility on your part and as great an honor to me as the washing of your apostles' feet. If I should decline this greatest sacrament out of fear, I "would have no part with you," according to your own word. And you insist on the necessity of my partaking of the bread: "Unless you eat the flesh of the Son of Man and drink his blood, you shall not have life in you. He who eats my flesh and drinks my blood has life everlasting and I will raise him up on the last day" (John 6:54–55). Lord, you made my whole life dependent on this holy sacrament.

I could have no spiritual life at all without it. Now is the time for me to meditate carefully on your promises and your command. What I am about to receive is not a reward for my own excellence, nor is it the product of the finest human invention. Here is infinitely more than man's work; it is the most personal condescension of the divine love and mercy. Small and weak as we are, God, the all-powerful Creator of the universe, makes us creations in his divine image, and then sharers of his own family table in the most real and complete sense. This is surely beyond our power to comprehend or explain. We can only accept the privilege with deepest gratitude and strive all our lives to grow in appreciation of it. To us, as to his dearest children, Jesus says, "I am the vine, you are the branches. He who abides in me, and I in him, he bears much fruit: for without me you can do nothing."

It is not only an invitation; it is a warning that I cannot dare to refuse it. Now is the most important activity of the day, for it is not myself acting; it is Jesus Christ in me. Nor have I any free choice in the matter. To reject total surrender to this great invitation is to reject the glory of my whole nature. For in Jesus Christ we are no longer mere creatures; we are sons of the Most High, surpassingly beautiful in the supernatural privilege he gives us, and utter nothingness without it.

So I am caught, Lord; captive to the most glorious design of love. The invitation is far above my merits, but I cannot decline, for I am of no value, of no account, of no life if I do not accept it.

What can I do, then? I must assent, but with the deepest reverential fear. Like Moses I must fall down on my face, for this is infinitely holy ground; like Isaias I must cry, "Woe is me, for I am a man of impure lips"; like John the Baptist I must know that I am not worthy to lossen the strap of your sandal, and I have no power to cleanse myself. "I will take the bread of heaven," then, but with fear "I will call upon the name of the Lord."

*Prayer: Lord, I believe and confess that you are in truth the Son of God. Permit me to share today in the mystery of your holy ban-*

*quet. I partake of your sacred mysteries, but may it not be to my sentence of damnation; no, let it be to the spiritual renewal of my soul and body.*

(Communion Prayer, Melkite Eucharistic Liturgy)

# 54.

## LORD, I AM NOT WORTHY

LORD, I AM NOT WORTHY THAT YOU SHOULD COME UNDER MY ROOF:
BUT ONLY SAY THE WORD AND MY SOUL WILL BE HEALED.

*So Jesus went with them. And when he was now not far from
the house, the centurion sent friends to say to him, 'Lord, do not
trouble thyself, for I am not worthy that thou shouldst come under
my roof; this is why I did not think myself worthy to come to thee.
But say the word, and my servant shall be healed. . . .' Now when
Jesus heard this, he marvelled, and turning to the crowd that fol-
lowed him, said, 'Amen I say to you, not even in Israel have I
found such great faith.' (Luke 7:6–7, 9)*

In how many ways, Lord, I am unworthy! I ought to be like
a dying man each time I come to receive you; a dying man knows
himself as he truly is, sees himself at last in some measure as God
sees him; no hypocrisy, no veneer, no excuses.

I am human (I hope) with an intelligence that automatically
passes judgment on many things daily. I have learned to discern
values, to pursue good and reject evil, to take difficult and drastic
measures at times according to judgments made. This is what
the centurion understood when he said sincerely, "Lord, I am not
worthy to have you enter my house."

Now I stand before you, face to face, my God. What an appalling

sight! Promises I made you—where are they? Broken, ruined, dis-
carded, gathering dust. The power I had in my hands to do good if
I had been a real Christian—where is it? Decayed from lack of use.
The duties I neglected, the good example I ignored, the love I per-
verted, the sympathy I denied—all these gaping wounds accompany
me to your holy table. If your charity resembled mine, Lord, you
would have fled already at the thought of my approach.

But you knew what manner of men and women would come to
receive you; you knew what thoughtless irreverence would accompany us. You have indeed "loved us with an everlasting charity,
drawing us mercifully into your presence."

I am one with my brothers and sisters in Christ, who are gathered in this church with me. If ever that should be clear to me, it
is now, as we approach your Eucharistic table together, We are
surely one in Christ. By your sacred Body and Blood we are "gathered together in the Lord." Here is not only the sacrament of personal holiness; it is the great sacrament of unity, the great reality
that makes us one, that gives us a necessary part with one another.
Christians cannot be cut off from one another and yet be Christians—or can Christ be torn asunder?

No, as he insisted, he and the Father are one, and we who are received by him must be one in him. It is he who invites us and receives us; it is not we who do the inviting. Therefore, Lord, we must
accept the invitation on your terms. It is an invitation of love, love in
the fullest sense, the all-embracing love of your whole Mystical
Body.

I approach the sacrament of unity and charity. The greatest ob-
stacles to my receiving it worthily or absorbing its grace are my bar-
riers against charity. There is no lack of charity in you, Lord, nor
in the grace you give me. But I am not a fit receptacle; my selfishness, my petty grudges, my lack of concern for the spiritual and
material welfare of my neighbor, my prejudices and secret hatreds,
my desire for self-preferment—these are so many punctures through
which your grace drains away, almost as soon as I receive it.

*Prayer: Turn your face away from my sins, Lord; look rather at the sacrifice I offer to you in atonement for them. The holy offering and the Lamb have much greater weight than my sins. It was because of my iniquities that your most loved Son was cruelly pierced by nails and spear. But behold the greatness of his suffering to make reparation to you! Through his Passion life is restored to me. Praise to the Father, who sacrificed his dear Son for our redemption. Homage to the Son, who gave up his life on the cross and won the blessing of life for us. Gratitude to the Holy Spirit, who initiated the mystery of our salvation and brought it to completion. O most high Trinity, shed your mercy on all of us. By your compassion, which forgave the good thief on the cross, forgive us, too, Son of God, and grant us mercy.*

*(Prayer of the Elevation, Malankarese Liturgy)*

# 55.

## TO LIFE ETERNAL

THE BODY OF OUR LORD JESUS CHRIST PRESERVE MY SOUL TO LIFE ETERNAL. AMEN.

*I say to you, he who believes in me has life everlasting. I am the bread of life. Your fathers ate the manna in the desert, and have died. This is the bread that comes down from heaven, so that if anyone eat of it he will not die. (John 6:47–50)*

Jesus gave very prominent emphasis in his words, actions, and miracles to the doctrine of the Eucharistic bread. In his lengthy discourse on the subject, recorded by St. John in his gospel (chapter 6), he stressed a special relationship between the heavenly bread and the resurrection to eternal life. The whole sequence of the instruction reveals the Eucharist as the bread that gives life—eternal life. Hence Holy Communion fortifies and prepares our human nature for the vision of God in heaven, especially in conjunction with the resurrection of our bodies.

The circumstances of the miracle of the loaves suggest such a meaning. Crowds of people have been listening to the words of Jesus; they have left behind the comforts of their homes; they have come out to a mountain-side for "the one thing necessary"—hearing God's message of salvation. But they are human; men, women, and children with bodily needs. Jesus "cannot send them home fasting, for they will faint along the way." He must give them something to strengthen them along their way—their way home—as they carry with them the words of God they have heard. Notice the clear suggestion of the Holy Eucharist and its purpose: we need nourishment to keep us from falling down in the journey of life. Jesus then works the miracle of the bread, to provide the strength his people need. In consequence, they proclaim him the great Prophet who was promised the world, and they follow him, seeking more bread, "Lord, give us this bread always."

Then Jesus prepares them to hear his teaching on the heavenly bread, a supernatural food to give spiritual nourishment and prepare men for the final resurrection. They should "not labor for the food that perishes, but for that which endures unto life everlasting," and the Son of God will provide that food. He introduces the subject by insisting that faith is necessary: "This is the work of God, that you believe in him whom he has sent."

Finally the doctrine of the Eucharist is given in full: Jesus himself is the bread of life; it is the Father's will that his flesh and blood be given to nourish men and to be their assurance of resurrection on the last day. Those who eat the bread of which Jesus speaks, are consuming his sacred Body and Blood, and therefore they live in him and he lives in them. His listeners object: "How can this man give us his flesh to eat?" But Jesus does not withdraw any part of his statement: "Unless you eat the flesh of the Son of Man and drink his blood, you shall not have life in you. . . . He who eats of this bread shall live forever." Many of his followers leave him because of this mysterious promise, but Jesus does not retract. He insists that "the spirit gives life; the flesh profits nothing," and he asks his apostles to make the decision between faith and rejection. Peter expresses their faith, and Jesus accepts it, indicating that one of them, Judas, does not believe.

Thus the promise is made, clear and complete. At the Paschal Supper, the promise is fulfilled, the instruction is given, Jesus consecrates the bread and commands his apostles, the Church, to continue this in his memory and according to the doctrine he had already explained at Capharnaum, as "the words of eternal life."

*Prayer: Lord, we ask you that our bodies may be blessed by your sacred body and our souls brought to new life by your grace-giving blood; may this win us pardon of our sins and atonement for our evil inclinations, Lord and God of us all. Praised may you be for all eternity.*

(*Communion Prayer, Maronite Liturgy*)

# 56.

## WHAT CAN I GIVE?

WHAT SHALL I GIVE THE LORD IN RETURN FOR ALL HIS GOODNESS TO ME? I WILL TAKE THE CHALICE OF SALVATION, AND INVOKE THE LORD'S NAME. I WILL CALL UPON THE LORD WITH WORDS OF PRAISE; I SHALL BE SAFE FROM MY ENEMIES. THE BLOOD OF OUR LORD JESUS CHRIST PRESERVE MY SOUL TO LIFE ETERNAL. AMEN.

*How shall I make a return to the Lord for all the good he has done for me? The cup of salvation I will take up, and I will call upon the name of the Lord; my vows I will pay to the Lord in the presence of all his people. Precious in the eyes of the Lord is the death of his faithful ones. . . . O Lord, to you will I offer sacrifice of thanksgiving, and I will call upon the name of the Lord. (Psalm 115:3–8)*

*You know that you were redeemed from the vain manner of life handed down from your fathers, not with perishable things, with silver or gold, but with the precious blood of Christ, as of a lamb without blemish and without spot. (I Peter 1:18–19)*

What can I do to repay Christ for the tremendous value he has set upon my soul? The more a friend does for me, the greater value he sets upon me; and thus it becomes more and more impossible for me to make any return to him that is adequate. Where can I begin to repay this benefactor, who first created me, then provided me with all the blessings of life—the air, the fruits of the earth to feed me, the waters to quench my thirst, the beauties of nature to delight my eyes, the talents to become a creator myself—and then personally gave his own blood to save me from my sins? How does one begin to show gratitude to so generous a father and friend?

How is it that he sets so great a value on us, who are such lowly creatures? We have earthly friends who set value on us, but how often it is in terms of how much cash lines our pockets! Or else they inquire as to our reputation, the quality of our family and our position. Or, if they are proud to be "democratic," they may overlook cash and reputation, but they ask, "What can you do?" They will value us as their friends if we produce, if we give promise of becoming "friends worth having."

There is no need to be sarcastic about these questions, Lord, for if asked by the right people, they have great significance. Not as the world asks them, but as the world's Creator and Master asks them. These were the very questions considered and answered by the Son of God when he determined his plan of redemption.

"How much are they worth?" He answered that, in his eternal wisdom, with another question, a greater one: "What can a man give in exchange for his soul?" The meaning is clear: no price is too high when it concerns your immortal soul, your precious spirit which was created for everlasting joy.

"How much are they worth?" You answered that, Jesus, with far more than words; you answered it by redeeming us with your own most precious blood. "You are worth every last drop of the blood of the Son of God. What price shall you put on the divine blood? Can it be exchanged for gold or rubies or diamonds?" Indeed, Lord, your blood cannot be bought for the price of the universe itself.

"What is the value of their family and their position?" Who can set a price on the family of God? Are we not adopted into your divine family through baptism? Are we not called the sons of God? What better family connections could we desire? Do not all earthly privileges and ranks pale beside the privilege of baptism?

"What can they do? What return can they make?" Is not this the

question we must ask ourselves again and again? Can we forget our
ingratitude to the Son of God, who set so high a price, so exalted a
dignity on our weak nature, that he did not hesitate to give his
precious blood for us? "What can we do?" All our lives ought to
be spent asking that question: "What can we do? Nothing, without
him. Everything, with him: everything in our power to bring ourselves and all those around us to love him, to imitate his love, to
keep so close to him that not one of those precious souls for whom
he bled shall be lost!"

Each time that we leave the church after taking part in the Holy
Sacrifice of the Mass, we must repeat that question over and over:
"What return shall I make to the Lord for all his goodness to me?"

*Prayer: Let us thank him together, we who by the generous grace
of the Holy Spirit have been made fit to approach him, to receive the
sacred, sublime, heavenly mysteries that give us life. Praised may he
be for his unutterable gift.*

(*Communion Hymn, Chaldean Liturgy*)

# 57.

## HOLY COMMUNION

MAY THE BODY OF OUR LORD JESUS CHRIST KEEP YOUR SOUL, BRING-
ING IT TO LIFE ETERNAL.

*And while they were at supper, Jesus took bread, and blessed and
broke and gave it to his disciples and said, 'Take and eat; this is my
body.' (Matthew 26:26)*

*And saying, 'Behold, I come to do thy will, O God,' he annuls
the first covenant in order to establish the second. It is in this 'will'
that we have been sanctified through the offering of the body of
Jesus Christ once for all. (Hebrews 10:10)*

> By being born, he gave himself to us as a companion,
> At his supper, he gave himself as our spiritual food,
> In dying, he gave himself as the price of our ransom,
> Reigning in heaven, he gives himself as our reward.

This quatrain, a free translation of a stanza of the *Verbum Super-
num,* Eucharistic hymn from the Roman breviary, expresses beautifully how the Son of God made himself a gift to us. He gave himself by joining our human race; he gave himself further to be our
food for all time while the earth lasts, by making himself the living
bread to nourish us with life—spiritual and eternal; he gave up his

life to be our ransom payment; he gives himself to us as our perfect fulfillment in heaven, our "eternal rest" in the sense that our desires shall rest content, since he is the complete happiness which the human soul seeks.

When Elias the prophet had outwitted and destroyed the false prophets of Baal, Jezabel, Queen of Judea, plotted his death. She had already killed many prophets of Israel's God, Yahweh, and now she sent a message to Elias: "The gods punish me as I deserve, if I have not made an end of you by this time tomorrow." Elias, knowing that his life was really in danger, fled southward into the desert. After a day's journey, exhausted and suffering hunger and thirst, he prayed God to take his life. He slept fitfully, sinking towards death. Then an angel awoke him with the command, "Arise and eat." There on the stone where Elias lay was a mysterious bread and a vessel of water. "He ate and drank, and he fell asleep again. The angel of the Lord came again and touched him and said, 'Arise, eat, for thou hast yet a great way to go.' So he arose and ate and drank, and walked in the strength of that food forty days and forty nights, unto the mount of God, Horeb" (3 Kings 19:6–8).

What a beautiful parable of our life with its trials and discouragements, and the strength afforded us by the bread of heaven. We are Elias; we have conquered the false prophets of Baal by our faith, received in baptism. But Jezabel, symbol of Satan, the adversary, who has killed others of the faithful before us, plots against our spiritual life. The world is full of temptation and dangers of many kinds; we wander through its deserts. Often, exhausted from the struggle, suffering a deep sense of separation from God, we are near despair. Seldom do we find friends to help us in this wilderness. But as we sleep there are messengers from God, saying "Arise and eat." The bread of life is laid out for us; we need only rise up and take it. And "in the strength of that food" we shall travel safely to the mountain of God. The trip may be long and dangerous, but if we eat of this bread we shall "have life in us," and we shall arrive, and ascend the mountain of God, and like Elias, we shall see God and speak with him.

Like the disciples on the journey to Emmaus, we shall have the Son of God as our companion, disguised at first, but known in "the breaking of the bread." He becomes our food, strengthening our bodies and souls for the glory of resurrection. He is a very special food: a sacrifice of atonement, which as it is received also cleanses us, washes away sin; we are accompanied in the journey through the desert by a bread that perfects us as we ascend the mountain of God. There, as we meet him face to face, we will say like the disciples, "Were not our hearts burning within us, as he accompanied us on the way?"

*Prayer: The servant of God receives of the thrice-holy and sacred Body and Blood of our Lord, God, and Redeemer, Jesus Christ, for the pardon of his sins and eternal life. Amen. This has touched your lips; it will wash away your offenses and cleanse you of your evil deeds.*

*O God, give salvation to your people and grant blessings to your children.*

*We have been shown the light which is true; we have been given the Spirit from heaven.*

(*Communion Prayers, Ruthenian Liturgy*)

# 58.

## WITH THE WHOLE MIND

LORD, GRANT THAT WHICH WE HAVE TAKEN WITH OUR MOUTH MAY BE
TAKEN WITH OUR WHOLE MIND; SO THAT THE GIFT RECEIVED IN EARTHLY
DAYS MAY BE A HEALING REMEDY FOR ETERNAL YEARS.

*The God of our fathers raised Jesus, whom you put to death,
hanging him on a tree. Him God exalted by his right hand to be
Prince and Savior, to grant repentance to Israel and forgiveness of
sins. (Acts 5:30–31)*

*Therefore to the Gentiles also God has given repentance unto
life. (Acts 11:18)*

The "gift received in earthly days" is to be a "healing remedy"
that will change us, make us perfect and worthy "for eternal years."
So powerful is the last and perfect gift of Jesus to the world. Of all
gifts, this one was the greatest in history, the one most often given.
This very day the words "This is My Body" were said in 500,000
churches around the world.

Why did Jesus give us this bread? His own life answers the question: his perfect sacrifice, his boundless love and purity and charity;
he could stay with us in the bread of life; he could continue his sacrifice, his coming to earth, his offering himself to save us. We say in
the Credo: "I believe . . . in Jesus Christ, who for us men and for
our salvation came down from heaven and was made man. . . ." We

might add, "and for us men and for our salvation, he stayed with us in the Holy Eucharist."

Yet after all these centuries of the perfect gift, how many of us receive that gift without receiving the spirit in which it was given to us! The Prayers after Holy Communion remind us that Jesus gave us himself in the Bread in order that he might transform us. He changed the bread into himself, so that he himself might *change us!* We read stories—both legends and histories—of how an experience or even a dream has changed people. And how much more this sacrament should change us!

One beautiful story of such a change of mind is *The Vision of Sir Launfal,* the knight who was about to go out in search of the Holy Grail. A noble journey, a worthy search; unfortunately, Sir Launfal was young and selfish; he did not understand in what spirit we are to search for Christ. He had despised Christ in the beggars that came to his own gate. He had something important to learn: the Holy Chalice was not a mere curiosity; it was a way of life, by which Jesus wished we should be *changed.* Such is the meaning of this prayer: "What we have taken with our mouth must be taken with our whole mind."

The night before he was to set out on his search, Sir Launfal had a dream. He saw himself as an old man, returning from his journey, a lifetime of fruitless searching. He had not found the treasured chalice. Now he was old, sick, weak, poor; he had lost his armor; one kind person had clothed him, and this apparel was now beggars' rags. It was winter, cold and harsh. Launfal saw the Christmas lights in his castle, but others lived there now. They would not remember him. The servants at the gate did not recognize him; he was thrown out into the snow. A beggar came up to him, asked for a cup of water and a slice of bread. How changed Launfal was! He had suffered, he had learned. Far from the pride and selfishness which had once made him despise the poor, he now gave the beggar his last crust, and with his bare hands broke the ice to fetch his guest some clear water.

Suddenly there was no more beggar; Launfal looked close. . . . It was Christ. And now the vision spoke:

> In many lands, without avail,
> Thou hast spent thy life for the Holy Grail;
> Behold, it is here—this cup which thou
> Didst fill at the streamlet for Me but now—
> The Holy Supper is kept indeed
> In what we share with another's need;
> Not what we give but what we share—
> For the gift without the giver is bare;
> Who gives *himself* with his alms feeds three—
> Himself, his hungering neighbor, and Me.

The story of Sir Launfal ends triumphantly: the dream and the vision have so changed the knight that the love of Christ fills his castle, and his charity is such that "the castle gate stands open now, and the wanderer is welcome to the hall"—

> And there's no poor man in the North Countree
> But is lord of the earldom as much as he.

The "temporal gift" of the vision became for Sir Launfal the "eternal remedy" of his soul. Should not the great gift of the Eucharist be all the more "a healing remedy for eternal years" in our souls? Is it not the sacrament of unity and charity? Are not the deeds of unity and charity "the return" that we must make "to the Lord for all he has given us"?

Another parallel appears between the parable of Sir Launfal and Holy Communion. Commentators tell us that St. Paul's warning to the early Christians against "eating unworthily" and thus "eating and drinking judgment" to oneself refers to the selfish attitude of the rich toward the poor at the Christian banquet. Those who had much of this world's goods stuffed themselves, while they allowed the poor to go hungry. It was particularly this lack of charity that St.

Paul condemned as making Christians unworthy of eating the Body and Blood of the Lord.

"What return shall I make to the Lord?" That of whole-hearted charity. Then I receive Christ not only "with the mouth," but "with the whole mind." With that change of mind I will be "putting on the Lord Jesus Christ" and "doing away with the old man" in me.

*Prayer: We give you thanks, Lord, for calling sinners to yourself, for asking sinful men to be your disciples, for disregarding the judgment that stood against us, for repealing that judgment in your mercy; the doom is abolished by our conversion and by your revelation of yourself. We give you thanks for allowing us to partake of your body and blood. Grant us your blessing; we are your people, and ask that our portion may be with the body and blood of your only Son. Through him let praise and honor be yours today and always, for all ages to come. Amen.*

### (Communion Prayer from the Early Church)

# 59.

## NO TRACE OF SIN

MAY YOUR BODY WHICH I HAVE RECEIVED, LORD, AND YOUR BLOOD
WHICH I HAVE CONSUMED BE UNITED TO MY INNERMOST BEING; GRANT
THAT NO TRACE OF SIN MAY REMAIN IN ME, SINCE YOUR PURE AND HOLY
SACRAMENTS HAVE RENEWED ME. YOU LIVE AND REIGN FOREVER AND
EVER. AMEN.

*In him we have redemption through his blood, the remission of
sins, according to the riches of his grace. This grace has abounded
beyond measure in us in all wisdom and prudence, so that he may
make known to us the mystery of his will . . . to re-establish all
things in Christ, both those in the heavens and those on the earth.
(Ephesians 1:7–10)*

How often the New Testament writers tell us that Jesus "shed his
blood for the remission of our sins." This does not mean that he
merely wanted to give us the good feeling that we could forget our
past, that the evil deeds we committed made no difference, or that
because of Christ's sacrifice our perfection required no work on our
part. Rather, he gave us hope that we could repair the damage we
had done, that cooperating with his grace and sharing the offering
he made of himself, we could begin to wipe away the traces of sin.
He gave us the assurance that when we realized how evil and sinful
we were, we need not and we must not sink into despondency.

In the madness of despair over her guilt, Lady Macbeth is heard muttering, "What, will these hands ne'er be clean? . . . Here's the smell of the blood still. . . . What's done cannot be undone." She has lost hope in the possibility of deliverance from her sin. She sees her soul a ruin, "in darkness and in the shadow of death," and in that pagan darkness commits suicide.

There is no doubt that the beauty and peace of innocence is shattered by sin. But must the marred soul be blackened by the false doctrine of despair? No repair? "What's done cannot be undone. . . ." Why not? Was it not the life-work of the Divine Redeemer to undo sin and guilt? Is it not the constant and insistent teaching of Holy Scripture, Old Testament as well as New, that reparation is the chief concern of the people of God?

"What's done is done—now it must needs be undone." Such is the Christian's way of remorse. Not fruitless, crushing grief, but "bringing forth fruit worthy of repentance." Christian life on earth is a blessed blending of joy with sorrow, of hope with regret, of love increased by the memory of past hatreds.

Wherever Jesus went during his public life, wherever he worked miracles to heal the sick and suffering, his first concern was always, "Take heart, son. Your sins are forgiven." He read minds and hearts; he knew our shame and sorrow. He had come to find what was lost, to rebuild what had fallen to ruin. His forgiveness said to us, "What's done is done, but I shall undo it, and I shall give you countless opportunities to undo it with me and because of me. Every good work, every gesture of love for me, every thought of sorrow and reverence, every action of true charity, every self-denial, every holy thought and generous deed shall undo the evil."

Most especially, his sacred presence cleanses us of evil. We do not receive his Body and Blood because we are really worthy; we receive him in order to become more worthy. With the strength of his sacrament at our side, we can work effectively at reparation. With him "united to my innermost being," the foundation is laid for removing "every trace of sin." We must reject the false conviction that old sinful habits can no longer be conquered. Every Holy Com-

munion, every new resolution and effort, every movement of re-
sistance to old weaknesses, every prayer and generous desire is a
true sign of progress, a deepening of the new habit of grace.

> Prayer: *Christ our sacrifice has been shared among us. Alleluia!*
> *He nourishes us with his sacred body, and his blood he*
> *sheds for us. Alleluia!*
> *Come near to the Lord and be illumined by his light.*
> *Alleluia!*
> *Taste and see how gracious is the Lord. Alleluia!*
> *Praise the Lord in his heavenly kingdom. Alleluia!*
> *Glorify him in the highest of heavens. Alleluia!*
> *Worship him, all his angels. Alleluia! Adore him, all his*
> *powers. Alleluia!*

**(Communion Hymn, Armenian Liturgy)**

# 60.

## CLOSING PRAYER

THE LORD IS WITH YOU. AND WITH YOUR SPIRIT. LET US PRAY. . . .

*And the spirit of God came upon Azarias . . . and he said, 'Hear ye me, Asa, and all Juda and Benjamin: The Lord is with you, because you have been with him. If you seek him, you shall find, but if you forsake him, he will forsake you.' (2 Chronicles 15:2)*

*And may the Lord of peace himself give you everlasting peace in every place. The Lord be with you all. (2 Thess. 3:16)*

The closing greetings ("The Lord is with you") and the closing prayers are well suited to the nature of the Mass. The Lord is indeed with us now; we have offered his sacrifice, we have joined ourselves in intentions and actions with the Son of God made man, we have united ourselves with him in receiving his body and blood. If the Lord is not with us now, it is not likely that he is at any other time.

The Postcommunion prayers vary with the feast and season. But they all carry the theme, "May this holy communion have on us the effect for which the Lord intended it." As we have meditated, our Lord's expressed intention was that our union with him in the Eucharist would make us strong with his life, and prepare us little by little for the infinitely brilliant vision of heaven and glorification of ourselves. This preparation is, of course, the Church's aim for us in this world; it is her very reason for existing. She is interested in the affairs of this world, and she must be, but to the extent that they are sanctified by God to contribute to our spiritual fulfillment and happiness through eternity. The Church is God's extension into time; she exists to lead us through time into timeless bliss. She does not ignore our temporal life, for it is here that our eternal life begins; it is here and now that we must "become a fountain springing up into everlasting life."

"Grant us, Lord God, that as we unite in celebrating the birth of our Lord Jesus Christ by these mysteries, so by a worthy life on earth we may become fit to share his company in heaven." (Postcommunion of Christmas) This prayer from the Christmas Midnight Mass is similar to that of the third Mass on that feast: "Almighty God, we ask that the newly-born Savior who brings about our rebirth to God's life may bring us to eternal life forever."

"Lord, grant that in heaven we may fully enjoy your divine beauty; a fulfillment which is now foreshadowed when we receive your precious Body and Blood." (Postcommunion, Feast of Corpus Christi)

We ask in the final prayer that the result of our part in the Mass may be "out of this world." It is the joyous privilege and awesome responsibility of the Church to make us ready for a happiness which is "out of this world."

There are three steps to this perfect world, through which we who aspire to it must pass. Each of them might be called a death, and it might be called a resurrection as well. The first is our death to sin in this world; we must die to selfish and sinful attachments that keep us from God. It is a resurrection, too, out of the sordid misery and frustration of evil.

The second step is death itself, death in the flesh, that deliverance from this mortal body which we see with our eyes, which takes us "out of this world." It is a resurrection, too, for the man of God who has rightly understood this life as a preparation, a growth and development into the perfection of the second and greater life.

The third step is the cleansing deliverance effected in Purgatory, where the final preparation for life and the final death to evil and all its sad consequences in our souls are mercifully supplied by God. Through all these steps we remain members of the Body of Christ, gradually purified to perfection.

Holy Communion does not separate us from our fellowmen any more than God himself does. Nor is it a substitute for our duties to our community. Rather, it is the strength we need in our labors, the purpose we need in our activities, the companion we need on our journeys. Our Lord said, "Come to me, all you who are burdened with labors, and I will refresh you." He did not say, "And I will excuse you, or deliver you, or take you away from your labors." No, that he will not do until the last moment on earth has come. He brings us the bread of heaven that we may have full life in ourselves, not that we may escape life. Hence our union with Jesus in this sacrament is not a substitute for duties; it deepens and enlarges our duties very much. Christ comes to us that we may be all the more conscious of our neighbor, all the more zealous to spread his kingdom on earth, all the more fortified to "restore all things in Christ." For as we share him at the Eucharistic table with our fellow Christians, so we must share him everywhere, with all the world.

*Prayer: He has favored us with the grace of the divine Spirit through our Lord Jesus Christ; he has invited us to his kingdom and requested that we partake of his eternal and boundless joy; he said to his holy disciples, "Believe me, whoever eats my flesh and drinks my blood lives in me and I live in him; I will bring him to resurrection on the last day; he will not come to a sentence of doom, but I will lead him straight from death to everlasting life." May he bless this congregation, may he direct our community and cleanse the people here, who with us have partaken with gladness in the sublime and strengthening and vivifying mysteries of God. May the life-giving sign of the Lord's cross be impressed upon us and save us from evil.*

(Final Prayer and Blessing, Chaldean Liturgy)

# 61.

## FORGIVENESS AND BLESSING

Be pleased, Holy Trinity, with the humble tribute of my service. Unworthy as I am, may the sacrifice which I have offered in the presence of your majesty be acceptable in your sight. May it obtain your merciful forgiveness for me and for all in whose behalf I offered it. Through Christ our Lord. Amen.

May almighty God, the Father, the Son, and the Holy Spirit bless you. Amen.

*Having therefore a great high priest who has passed into the heavens, Jesus the Son of God, let us hold fast our confession. For we have not a high priest who cannot have compassion on our infirmities, but one tried as we are in all things except sin. Let us therefore draw near with confidence to the throne of grace, that we may obtain mercy and find grace to help in time of need. (Hebrews 4:14-16)*

As we meditate on this final prayer of the Mass, we recall how often during the liturgy of the sacrifice we have begged God to accept our offering in atonement for our sins. The thought of our need for forgiveness and our need to present a pleasing gift recurs frequently and emphatically. It is well that it does: we Christians are far too glib and glossy on the nature of God's forgiveness. We seek pardon for our sins—and even drag our feet in doing that!—then presume without further concern that all is paid and abolished.

This is hardly the mind of Christ, from whom we receive forgiveness. Christ, who spoke no words of pardon unless he saw faith, admission of guilt, and sorrow, spoke consistently in parables that warned, "thou wilt not come out from that prison until thou hast paid the very last mite," and "unless you do penance, you will all perish in the same manner," and "that servant who knew his master's will, and did not make ready for him and did not act according to his will, will be beaten with many stripes," and "of everyone to whom much has been given, much will be required." (Luke 12 & 13)

Words of sorrow are uttered, the sin is confessed, the prayer of penance is said, but the evil habit is not so easily uprooted and the debt is not so easily paid. What can we say of a contrition that plans no reparation and takes no action to conquer the sinful weakness? It is one evil to despair of forgiveness, but it is another evil to presume that with a word—even the word of absolution—the danger of future falls is automatically removed. Christ Jesus sacrificed himself on the cross to redeem us from sin, but surely his strong words of warning and his serious demands for sacrifice imply a great amount of action on our part. "Not everyone who says to me, 'Lord, Lord,' shall enter the kingdom of heaven . . . but he who does the will of my Father. . . ."

Christ willingly forgave the sinful woman while the Pharisees were picking up stones to kill her, but Christ said to her, "Go now, and *sin no more*." To a paralytic, whom he forgave and favored with a miracle, Jesus said, "Sin no more, lest some worse thing befall thee."

When someone has offended us, you or me, and begs pardon, we are already saying within ourselves, "Let your actions show that you are sorry." We ought also to be saying within ourselves, "And so be it with me, Lord. I am asking your forgiveness continually. Let my actions show that I am sorry."

May this sacrifice which I have offered before you, O Lord, be ac-

ceptable in your sight. How can I make it more acceptable? Surely
by making it more fruitful, more effective, more meaningful in my
work today, in my environment this week, in my attitude towards
my neighbor—my family, my co-workers, my friends, my rivals, my
community, my country, and the world itself.

*Prayer: May the Lord bless us with peace and pardon of sins,
through the Body and Blood that has been given us. Give us strength
through your Holy Spirit to conquer every sinful force; we are confident in the power of your blessed, forgiving hand. Lead us away
from all evil deeds, and inspire us to every kind of good work.
Praise to him who has honored us with his sacred body and blood.
By virtue of the cross of Jesus Christ, we have been given grace and
life. We thank you, Lord, for the grace we have received from the
Holy Spirit.*

*(Final Prayer, Ethiopic Liturgy)*

# 62.

## AFTERTHOUGHT

*In the beginning was the Word, and the Word was with God: and the Word was God. . . . In him was life, and the life was the light of men. And the light shines in the darkness; and the darkness grasped it not. . . . He came unto his own, and his own received him not. But to as many as received him he gave the power of becoming sons of God; to those who believe in his name: Who were born not of blood, nor of the will of flesh, nor of the will of man, but of God. (Gospel of St. John 1:1, 4, 11–13)*

A popular American musical commentator was asked to describe very briefly what a symphony is. "Well," said he, "even people who hate classical music know that a symphony has four movements: *in, down, up,* and *out.*" The four simple words—one-syllable prepositions—do give a striking and imaginative summary, crude as it is, of the nature of a symphony. Does not the music move *in* hesitatingly, *down* majestically, *up* joyously, and *out* triumphantly?

Not much is learned about the Mass by suggesting that it is a musical or dramatic program, however embellished some High Masses may be. Yet those four small words may serve as a remarkable figure of the Holy Sacrifice. It is only a figure, for the Mass is too great to receive justice in a whole book, however large or however excellent. It is a happy figure, suggesting what we might do at Mass: in, down, up, out.

IN: that is the whole purpose of the first part of the Mass through the Offertory: to find our way IN to God. To get into the groove of thinking and feeling with God: feeling our unworthiness, our helplessness, our need for him. The Confiteor, the Kyrie Eleison: Lord, have mercy. We are not worthy to come in, but we must get in, so that we can hear his word and be enlightened. We come in to hear the lessons from Holy Scripture, and their application to us (the sermon). Then we go in with our offerings, the bread and wine. We offer them, knowing what they are to become; thus we go in to God with a little less shame.

DOWN: God has accepted us; at the words of the priest he comes down. "This is my Body." Behold how God comes down! Behold how small a piece of bread veils his mighty presence. See how the King of the Universe has emptied himself. But not without a purpose. He comes down that we may rise up.

UP: the third part of the Mass is the Communion. We are truly lifted up to heaven, to the height of God. If Christ comes down, humbles himself, stoops to us, all the more do we rise up, exalted, lifted to the height of union with him.

OUT: the closing prayers. We are to go out new men, strong in unity, deep in charity, full in wisdom. We go out prepared for life, with an understanding of its purpose, carrying in us the grace of Christ. We go out, but not to leave him. We go out to carry him with us.

Such, briefly, is the Mass: we in, Christ down; we up, Christ out with us to the corners of the earth.

"I have sent you out that you may bear fruit, and that your fruit will remain." The fruit is to remain, because we, like the disciples of Christ, are sent out to bear it anew. How frequently our Lord insisted that we must take his message to heart and make it bear fruit a hundredfold. His words must be incarnated in our lives, as they were in his. He assures us that by our fruits we will be judged.

If we examine a "fruit," we may ask, "How many sides are there to it—to a grapefruit or orange or apple or plum?" The answer: two sides—inside and outside. The answer indicates what our "fruit" of the Mass must be: both internal and external. Inside is the deep love that must be the core of our actions. Outside are the works done, which prove in fact that love and repentance in us are real. Like the inner core of fruit, which bears the life-seed of further fruit, our interior love for God assures us of continued external good works: the outer fruit will be reproduced again and again.

"Either tell us that the tree is sound and its fruit sound, or that the tree is withered and its fruit withered," said our Lord. "The test of the tree is in its fruit" (Matthew 12:33). The core of fruit without external covering will soon rot and waste away. Love that never expresses or exercises itself will soon deteriorate. On the other hand, of what value is a mere shell? With what disgust do we peel a piece of fruit to find its interior rotten! We were not asked to "bring forth peelings," works without a heart, without true inner meaning, without the inner force of grace.

"Go, you are dismissed," we are told at the end of Mass. The banquet is over; we are refreshed and strengthened; but we are not to squander what we have received. The bread of heaven was given us "that we may have life in us." We go out as we came in—followers of Christ, apostles and disciples. And to them, Jesus said, "I have chosen you and have appointed you that you should go out and bear fruit, and that your fruit should remain." (John 15:16)

*Prayer: Lord, preserve your people and grant blessings to your children; direct them and raise them up to life eternal; make them strong in sincere faith and reverence for the full length of their lives; inspire them with love for divine things and for the peace which exceeds understanding. . . . O King of Peace, Anointed One, Divine Master, fill us with your peace, for all kingship and power and grandeur belong to you forever. Amen. God the Almighty, Father, Son, and Holy Spirit bless you. Go forth in peace. Amen, for all time.*

(Final Prayer of the Coptic Liturgy)